Profit Improvement

in **7** steps…

…and in **227** actions

Tim Levey

DEDICATION

To Theresa and Rebecca

ACKNOWLEDGMENTS

Angela West for the cover design

Maria White (Miss Beady Eyes) for editing

James Cross and Mark Lloydbottom for the Inspiration

Barry Schimel CPA and Gary Kravitz – Authors of *All About Earnings* (Capital Books Inc. Virginia USA)

and my Partners at Reeves for their support

PREFACE

Welcome to this updated version of the book first published in
2004 by Hodder & Stoughton under the title 'Profit Improvement
in a Week'. This just goes to show that 'if you don't try, don't be
surprised if nothing happens'. Having had the ambition for
many years to get published, in my mind I was going to retire
before I set my mind to writing my novel, which would find its
way to a publisher and would sell modestly. The volume of the
sales was never the important thing – the getting it published
was.

Then I read somewhere that the chances of getting a novel
published was minimal, but that there was a much better chance
if the work was non-fiction. By that time I had spent the
previous 6 years at Reeves+Neylan working with James Cross in
researching a systematic way of improving profits that we
trademarked 'PROFIT*Plus*'. During that research I had bought
and read a number of books in Hodder's series of 'In a Week'
books. These all took a subject and split it into 7 parts so that the
reader could tackle one part per day, starting on Sunday and
finishing on the following Saturday. Luckily the publisher had a

section on their website where new authors were invited to pitch their work. So having spent some time planning how the 'PROFIT*Plus*' system, which by then had grown into 7 thick manuals, could be squeezed into 7 sections over 96 pages, I sent off an email saying that I thought there was a gap in their series. I couldn't quite believe it when they agreed!

The 'In a Week' series had been around for at least 10 years and a number of the titles had been updated over that period – what better opportunity was there? It all seemed too good to be true and, as it happened, I think that mine was one of the last books added to the series before Hodder decided that it had run its course and the entire series was taken out of print! There are still a handful of used copies out there in bookstores but, as the numbers have dwindled and the prices have gone up, the thought of getting the rights returned and publishing an updated copy came up.

Over the period since 2004, the business world has certainly gone through a great many changes. The answers to the question 'How do you improve profitability?' have kept changing but the question has remained the same. In turbulent times the most important part of the process has started with the 'Intentions Review' covered here in Step 3. As markets have moved and shifted around a business with sometimes breathtaking speed, the need to be conscious of the positioning, or the 'Intention', of a business has become of fundamental importance. Business owners who take their eye off that part of the market can find that suddenly it has disappeared.

So the bulk of the text is unchanged from the Hodder version – it is as relevant today as it was then.

However, in terms of what to call it, a new title was needed to differentiate this from the Hodder edition of 'Profit Improvement in a Week'. In any event there was no way that the reader could actually cover all of the ground required in one week, hence the more realistic title of 'Profit Improvement in 7 Steps'.

Also, to add to the original there's now a 'Part 2'. A fundamental part of the PROFIT*Plus* system was a collection of more than 200 different ways that businesses could implement to improve their profits. In its complete form it filled 3 thick lever arch files, but some years ago we condensed this down into a booklet that we used for promotional purposes. This booklet was used as the basis for Part 2 - 'Profit Improvement in 227 Actions'.

I hope that you enjoy it.

Tim Levey

PART ONE

PROFIT IMPROVEMENT
IN 7 STEPS

INDUCTION – PART ONE

In reality it's quite easy to improve the profits of any business, and see some positive effects on the profit line in under a week as well! Just go ahead and cut costs anywhere you like on Monday morning and by Friday afternoon you can probably point to higher profits.

But what about next week and the week after that? Randomly cutting costs can only be a short term approach in desperate circumstances. If that were the way to maximise profits over the long term then every business would do it. Experience suggests that businesses that do take this approach tend not to be around for very long. Our goal in this process is to go beyond random cost cutting and outline an approach to improving profitability over the long term.

Many businesses work hard to improve their profitability. In general, however, this will be through a disjointed collection of different projects which have probably been formulated in reaction to an urgent need or crisis. This book will explain how it is better to have some system that identifies and deals with issues before the need becomes urgent.

One new groundbreaking idea makes it possible to substantially improve the profits of a business. Unfortunately such ideas are few and far between. As an alternative to spending time looking for something that might not exist, all businesses could instead improve profits by turning their attention to a number of smaller areas in their operations.

This Profit Improvement Process has three key phases:
1. Information Gathering
2. Idea Generation
3. Implementation Guidance

The steps ahead

Step 1. We will define what is meant by Profit Improvement and explain why this process is more effective than just providing a list of general areas to look at.

Step 2. We will consider the importance of incentives in the process and suggest some alternatives to consider in preparation for different stages throughout the coming steps.

Step 3. The Information Gathering work starts by checking and reviewing the current direction of the business (its Intention).

Step 4. Analysing the business from a number of different perspectives will complete the Information Gathering. This will entail looking generally at the business and then going into more detail on issues that this identifies. The result will be a list of the key issues facing the organisation.

Step 5. The key issues for which there are no immediate solutions are now presented to the staff in a workshop setting. Their ideas for solutions are generated, discussed and captured in an Ideas Plan.

Step 6. For the project to be successful, the ideas agreed so far now need to be implemented as effectively and efficiently as possible. We will look at a structured approach to implementation that reduces the chance of costly failure.

Step 7. With the ideas now agreed, the improvement in those areas needs to be inspected and monitored if the momentum is to be kept going into the coming weeks and months.

STEP 1:
INTRODUCTION TO PROFIT IMPROVEMENT

We will start by looking at what 'profit' is. We will then look at three standard types of businesses and consider examples of how such businesses do not maximise the profit that they make. We will also consider the main reasons why suggestion schemes, which are a common tool in profit improvement, fail and therefore what needs to be in place for such an initiative to be successful.

It would be naive to suggest that businesses exist solely to make profits. People want more than that. However, businesses cannot exist long without making profits and generating money. This profit, or self-generated income, provides resources for expansion and reward for the risk that shareholders take on. You can live off previously generated profits or borrow in the short term, but long term you must somehow make a profit to remain viable.

To understand that there is more to Profit Improvement than cost cutting we need to start by defining what 'profit' is. The *Oxford English Dictionary* presents a technical definition as 'the excess of returns over outlay.' Immediately, therefore, we have 'increasing the returns' as an alternative to 'reducing the outlay'.

Retail and wholesale businesses

Such businesses have been in existence since the original days of bartering and are alive and well in any street market. You buy goods from one party (the outlay) and sell the same goods to a number of others (the returns). So long as you have sold the goods for more money than you paid, then you have made a profit.

Such businesses may try to maximise their profits by cutting their costs or getting as many customers as possible, but such tactics ignore two other ways of improving profitability:

- Increasing the value of each sale – by encouraging each customer to buy something else
- Increasing the frequency of sales – by encouraging each customer to return soon!

These two alternatives recognise that it is easier to sell to an existing customer than it is to find, and then sell to, a new customer.

Manufacturing businesses

In terms of a typical manufacturing business, its 'returns' will be the sales income that comes from despatching its products to customers. Its 'outlay' will come under two general headings of:

- Direct outlays in manufacturing the products such as raw materials, labour costs and factory costs (light, heat, etc)
- Other costs not directly related to the manufacturing such as sales and marketing costs, administrative costs and finance costs

Suppose, however, that the business you were in had low customer retention for your industry at 60%. You find that 5% of goods delivered are rejected and returned and that staff retention is also low at 50%. The accounts of the business may show that it is making a small profit, but investors require a greater return. While cost cutting can quickly reduce the outlays, it is often the case that the cuts will be made in areas that can make the results worse in the longer term. For example, cutting the marketing budget probably leads to an even lower sales income, and cutting production staff could increase the percentage of goods rejected by customers.

The root causes of the lost profits tend to be things such as:

- Materials being badly stored, so that purchase orders are made for items held in stock
- Unclear order instructions from the sales staff to the production staff
- Bottlenecks in the production process that are left unaddressed

These and many similar problems get lost in bigger numbers. It is difficult to see that sales income is lower than it could be, or that material and labour costs are higher than they could be. Then there is a knock-on effect in that other costs such as sales and marketing costs may be higher than they need to be to make up for the poor customer retention. Even worse, staff morale never improves as the profits are never high enough to generate the cash to re-invest in new equipment.

Service businesses
These businesses will be faced with a different set of issues from the manufacturing business, but the result will be the same. At the beginning there is a marketing process to make potential clients aware of the services on offer. At the end, money is banked and a follow up contract sought. Between these two there are many things that can get in the way to suppress profits. Often the job is not completed as fast as it could be, or is sometimes not even completed at all. Because productive staff tend to be by far the greatest cost, the main drains of profitability will be those that affect them.

These typically include:

- Inadequate planning of a job so that it is not completed as efficiently as possible
- A poor induction procedure for new employees, which means that it takes longer for them to generate profits
- Work being done by too high a grade of staff (under-delegation)
- Negative attitudes in the staff team which go unaddressed

While the main profit problems, as with the manufacturing business, get hidden in the 'cost of sales' line, in a service business they are more likely to be found in the 'staff costs' number.

The problem
Just from looking at these three different types of businesses, it can be seen that there are many reasons why profits are not maximised. With every business being unique, the degree to which each possible issue is a factor will differ. So with that background, how can there exist a single approach to Profit Improvement that can apply to all businesses?

The solution
For a long-term solution to Profit Improvement an approach is needed that recognises that every business is different, if it is to identify efficiently where the returns could be higher and the outlay lower. Just as the profitability of a business is determined by how well it performs a myriad of small tasks, so the profit can be improved effectively and ethically by addressing these many tasks. You could bring in an external consultant to find the solutions for you, but usually the answers are *inside* the business already.

This answer is clear when you go behind the technical definition of profit and recognise that the 'returns' and 'outlays' do not belong to separate worlds, but are interlinked. Profits (or losses) are the result of the levels of commitment, creativity, discipline, effort and energy of the *people* in the business. These people are often the biggest outlay of a business, but they also control most of the other outlays and have decisive influence over revenues and returns, if only by the level of customer care that they provide. With profits therefore being the result of human endeavour, any Profit Improvement Process needs to capture the ideas of those people who help to create it.

Who should be involved?

In attempting to improve the profits of a business, one problem is that too many people believe that only they know the solutions. Senior management, for example, often maintain that it is 'their responsibility' to improve the profits and are unwilling to share this. In the meantime, everyone down to the most junior person in a business believes that they know how to make improvements. Even the advisers of the business, be they the accountant or the bank manager, believe that they have something to contribute.

The secret of successful Profit Improvement is to use *everyone's* ideas and abilities to the greatest advantage. As many people as possible need to be able to contribute. The best ideas can then be agreed by consensus and swiftly put into practice. This needs to be done in a planned way, as the haphazard approach that most businesses take means that it will take longer to achieve an imperfect result.

Why do Suggestion Schemes fail?

Many businesses have tried and failed to seek ideas for improvement by getting all the staff together and asking them for their ideas. Others have avoided this direct approach by running a suggestion scheme. These tend to be started in a blaze of intensity but can quickly fizzle out.

9

The reasons for these failed attempts include:

- Staff are not prepared for the request for ideas
- Rewards to the staff for contributing ideas are non-existent or unclear
- The ideas are not recognised and valued by management
- There is no structured follow up with staff after the idea has been put forward
- Even the best ideas do not get put into practice

Any one of these could be enough to make the whole initiative fail, so the process needs to be robust enough to cover all of these issues.

The benefits and features of this Process
The process that will be followed has the benefit of ensuring that the many ideas generated that will improve profitability are implemented as efficiently as possible.

The features are that:

Before ideas are sought:
- Management is agreed upon the general direction of the business. This enables them to give a message to staff that focuses their efforts.
- A scheme that incentivises Profit Improvement is agreed, so that there is something in it for everyone who takes part. This will make the seeking and collecting of ideas easier, but more importantly the scheme should extend to the implementation of those ideas as well.

As ideas are sought:

- Many people in the business become involved, which means that teamwork is improved and more progress is made faster, particularly in implementing ideas.
- The ideas focus on the issues of your particular business, which is unique. This means that you do not get side-tracked looking for issues that may be common in other businesses or sectors, but not in your own.
- The ideas come from inside the business, which means that they have more chance of being adopted.

After the ideas have been collected:

- Responsibility for each idea is taken by one individual, who will not necessarily be from the management group.
- Each idea is supported by an estimate of the increase in profitability that will result.
- The overall plan is prioritised, so that resources can be directed at the most important issues.
- The implementation of projects is rigorously followed up, so that adjustments can be made if necessary.

Prerequisite for success

Of great importance to the success of a major Profit Improvement exercise is the mindset of the senior management of the business. At the very least they all need to have the intention of doing something positive. If they are truly unhappy about the present situation, even irritated and impatient for improvement, then so much the better. On the other hand, if management is feeling comfortable with performance and profits, then this process is unlikely to be of interest to them at the moment.

So - are you motivated enough to want to improve profitability? You can find out by answering the question "What would higher profits enable me to do?" The answers could be more salary or income, more funds to help you in retirement, the reduction or removal of debt finance, the ability to invest more in the business, or maybe to maximise the value of the business prior to it being sold. There must be compelling reasons for going ahead because, as with many processes, Profit Improvement means change, and change is difficult.

"Profit Improvement is the result of implementing ideas in a structured way."

This phrase sums up the key to success in the process!

A general test of your resolve before proceeding is to answer the questions on the next page.

If you score in the top half that is above 28 then you clearly have a positive attitude towards this and would benefit greatly from following the process through the steps. The higher your score, the more certain this is.

	1 = I strongly disagree 4 = I have no strong feelings 7 = I strongly agree						
	1	2	3	4	5	6	7
I am unhappy with the current profitability of the business							
I am prepared to do something positive about the problems that we face							
I do not think that staff are working together as a team							
I believe that there are opportunities that pass us by							
I find that once we decide to do something, it gets done							
I know that business could be done more efficiently							
I agree that the answers to improving profits are in the business somewhere							

Before you get too far....

Part of the process is to generate ideas and implement them, but if the business is working on too many other initiatives already, then you could only add to the problem. Many businesses have 'initiative indigestion', with very little ever getting done.

The first thing to do, before you get too far into the process, is to try to bring to completion, or at least clear from your desk, projects that are being worked on at the moment.

Make a list of all the initiatives that the business is working on and assess them in terms of the following:

- How complete are they? Estimate this as a percentage to give you an idea of how much work remains.
- Who is working on each one? Identify the person who is responsible.
- How important is each initiative? Grade this on a scale of 1 to 7, with 1 being vitally important and 7 being a waste of time.
- How much input is needed? Again on a scale of 1 to 7, with 1 being very little and 7 being massive.
- How much will the completion of the initiative increase the profits of the business?

Now spend some time assessing these initiatives. Divide them into the initiatives that you are working on and ones that others in business are working on. Should any of them be stopped because they are unworkable, or are past their useful date, or will not contribute to the performance and profitability of the business?

If the person responsible for doing many of these jobs turns out to be you, then question whether you are the right person. Could someone else be rewarded for taking initiatives on, so freeing up your own time?

Spend time now getting the worthwhile ones completed or at least on track. There is no need to clear all of the initiatives - otherwise you may never get started! Having done this you will be ready and prepared for the steps ahead!

Final preparations for the initiative
With these things taken care of, it is now time to put the plans in place for the next steps. The most important of these is to consider how you will let everyone in the business know that over this period there is going to be a 'Profit Improvement Process' for the business. Staff will be able to contribute more effectively if they are aware what will be happening in each step and where their help may be needed. An announcement that there will be rewards for helping the business should also go down well.

STEP 2:
INCENTIVE SCHEMES

Now an important foundation needs to be put in place before the detailed work can start.

The owner or the manager who wants to start this Profit Improvement Project has probably got a strong motivation of some sort. They will have decided, or at least hope, that the rewards for pursuing this process will be worth the time and cost involved. That will be enough if they plan to do all of the work themselves, but if they want to involve other people from the business in the exercise then there is a need to think about how it is planned to incentivise them.

Consideration needs to be given to rewards at each level of the process therefore:

- People need to open up about what is happening at the moment.
- You need to encourage them to come up with ideas.
- They then need to be encouraged to implement the best ideas.

Now your people should be encouraged that it is to their long-term advantage to make the organisation more profitable. It can be tempting to think that there is no need to incentivise staff and that they will be sufficiently motivated to assist. However, human beings in general have a need for recognition and reward, especially for special efforts, which is what the process will demand in the implementation stage.

If you already have a bonus scheme for staff that is related to the profitability of the business, then you have a head start. Staff should already be aware that they would be rewarded as a team should the business be more profitable. Letting them know that there will be an opportunity in the coming weeks to add to that bonus will get you a long way. All that you may need in addition is some individual incentives to complement this.

Possible incentives
The most obvious incentive is cash, but there are plenty of other options to consider:

Gift certificates
These could be particularly useful in rewarding individual ideas or contributions. If they are being used for larger rewards then ask the recipient to tell everyone what they spent the certificate on.

Donations to charity
You may have a charity that the entire business supports, or you may want to let each employee donate his or her reward.

Paid time off
The incentives do not need to be financial. With modern day living meaning that spare time is at a premium, paid time off could be valued more than money. It does, however, need to be made clear that this will be a one-off reward rather than a permanent entitlement.

Dinner out
This could be as individuals or as a group. You may want to do this anyway, in addition to any other rewards, to make sure the whole team gets something out of contributing.

Travel or holiday vouchers
These would be good for the larger reward of making the implementation happen, but not for smaller rewards.

Health club membership
Again, this could be for individuals or for a group. It may be something that is worth doing anyway, given the likely reduction in rates of absenteeism that results from staff being both physically and mentally healthier.

Entertainment tickets
A good idea, but they need to be handled with care. Will the entertainment that you chose be suitable for everyone? Different generations have different concepts of 'entertainment'.

Choosing the incentives

Not all incentive schemes work! A badly designed or implemented scheme can do more damage than good. The guidelines of a successful scheme are that it must be:

- Easy to install and operate
- Easily understood and perceived as fair by everyone
- Linked to the results required
- Given now rather than later

There is one other important factor to consider. There is nothing worse than spending a great deal of time and resources designing an incentive scheme to support the programme, only to find that people are not interested in the incentive and therefore are not minded to contribute. The only failsafe way to ensure that the rewards will have the required effect is to ask your team what they want.

This is the ideal opportunity to introduce the Profit Improvement Process to the business.

Communicate to them an outline of what is planned for the 7 steps, how you would like them to contribute and ask them what incentives they would like. They can either be presented with a list similar to the list of possible incentives shown previously or throw things open and give them a blank piece of paper. The team could surprise you by asking for something that you might never have thought of, but if they tell you it will really motivate them.

After the team have told you what incentives they value most, involve them in the design, development and implementation of the scheme. It has more credibility if they have had a hand in creating it. That way the result should be one that they understand and this will be a great advantage later in the period.

How much should the incentives be?

For each phase of the process there will need to be a different incentive scheme. You may not think it necessary to incentivise the Information Gathering stage - normally people are only too willing to have their say about what is happening at the moment and this may be the one phase where incentives are least required.

During the Ideas Generation phase, it is best to have several small incentives in place as these tend to be better than a few large ones. The unusual coins or notes in the currency are best, otherwise small gift certificates are good to hand out. When you reach the Implementation phase, it might be tempting to just go for a percentage of savings achieved. However, you may want to put a maximum limit on the sum payable for each idea, or offer a scale of fixed sums depending upon the improvement achieved. The advantage of agreeing fixed sums is that it limits the amount of discussion about the size of the gain.

General rules on incentives

Don't reward activities.
Do reward results.

Don't tamper with basic pay rates - keep them at competitive market levels.
Do use incentives to take pay to the higher end of the market.

Don't make promises that you cannot afford to keep.
Do fund incentives schemes from the funds that they generate.

Don't rely on individual incentives alone.
Do incentivise teams.

Don't make the scheme too complicated.
Do involve staff in the design of the scheme.

Final words on incentives

Be aware that the whole area of incentives is a minefield when it comes to taxation. As a general rule, gifts provided to an employee by reason of that employment are taxable and the tax authorities take a special interest in these arrangements.

Secondly, if you are doing this more than once then you will need to re-think the incentives each time. After a while any reward can lose its motivational power. It can get to seem like an entitlement and people will come to rely on it as part of pay.

Finally, now that the structure of incentives has been agreed, this should be published so that everyone in the business is clear about them.

STEP 3:
INTENTIONS REVIEW

Next you will start the work involved in gathering information
in order to work out where the business is at the moment and,
more importantly, where it should be heading. This has been
termed its 'Intention'.

The first objective is to review, test and if necessary revise the
current Intention of the business. If possible, this should be
done in a group with other key members of management.

Your present Intention
To start, write down where you believe the business is
currently heading in the long run. This will be 'the present
Intention of the business.'

This is a concept similar to a 'Mission' or 'Vision'. However, as
will be seen, its definition is more specific than either of these.
Missions and visions, which tend to be condensed into a
written statement, can be the result of many different

processes. At one extreme they can come in a blinding flash of inspiration to the business owner or Managing Director and they are presented to staff almost as a message from above.

There are clear reasons why missions and visions that come about in this way are, in hindsight, rarely successful. They tend to have been constructed in a vacuum of idealism, usually by just one person, who then has the difficult job of getting the buy-in of everyone else in the business. Should they later come back to analyse their business environment in more detail, very often there is not a good fit and the process goes back to the beginning to find a new vision.

Clearly, this is the wrong way round. How can anyone set missions and visions, or goals and strategies, without having a clear picture of where their business is at the moment?

At the other extreme, Missions and Visions can be the result of a lengthy period of analysis about where the business is at the moment and where it should be heading. Businesses can be examined from every conceivable angle to ensure that nothing is missed out and the exercise will cover both internal and external issues. Sometimes this analysis can go on over many months.

The problem with this latter approach is that *you* have a limited amount of time in which to get your direction formulated and agreed. What is needed is a quick strategy review that does not run the risk of getting stuck in the detail or paralysed by analysis.

The Intention of a business is defined as *the overall aim of the business, which demonstrates specifically how the business will meet the needs of its customers in the context of the marketplace.*

This highlights two fundamental parts of the question "where is the business now?":
- the business environment and climate; and
- the needs of the customers or clients.

If you think that this is too simplistic, then consider successful and profitable businesses that you know. You should find that, whether by luck or judgement, they do indeed provide a product or service that customers or clients want in sufficient volume for them to be successful and profitable. The market that they are operating in will be conducive to their success, or at least does not hinder it. Now think about some unsuccessful businesses that you know, or ones that were successful and then lost their way. See if one of these two parts is missing. If you believe that both parts are or were there when it was unsuccessful, then the answer is that the business struggled as a result of the internal operations of the business. We will address internal issues later. But first things first.....

If correctly constructed, the 'Intention' will be valuable later in the process, as it should:

- Make clear to staff just where the business is heading and how their efforts can help.
- Assist with the selection of the issues that need to be tackled for the business to achieve its Intention.
- Assist teams with prioritising the Profit Improvement ideas that come from the process.

So how was the Intention that you recorded as the first exercise?

Intention credibility test
Is the Intention customer or client orientated?

Is it still relevant in the current marketplace?

In the light of the above definition, are you still happy with it?

If you believe that your written Intention honestly passes the credibility test, then take a rest and prepare for the next step!

On the other hand, if what you have written was formulated some time ago or does not otherwise pass the credibility test, then it is likely to be in need of a reassessment.

Business environment and climate
Being inside a business can be likened to a ride in a raft through white-water. Miss the current and you are left paddling hard but going nowhere. Choose to ride where the current is dangerously strong and you risk plummeting down, out of control and heading for possible destruction. But getting the strength of current and the route right, you find that everyone can work together to get through the white-water in the fastest time and with the best results. Throughout the journey the occupants feel exhilarated.

So this part of the review is about testing the currents.

This will be tackled in two parts:

- Porter's Five Forces model, which considers the various types of competitive forces of which a business needs to be aware.
- Other key external factors that are likely to be outside the control of the business, but shape the business environment in ways that cannot be ignored.

The following questions should be answered as honestly as possible, giving as much detail as possible:

Porter's Five Forces

1. *Competition within the industry:* Rivalry between competitors can take many forms beyond price competition. Businesses can focus on after-sales service, product quality, and even safety. This competition tends to be more aggressive if the industry is not growing, has high fixed costs, is fragmented or sometimes when there are high growth rates that are attracting new competitors.
   So who are your key competitors at the moment? Where are they based or is this irrelevant? Which markets are they focusing on and what appears to be their strategy?

2. *Customer:* Customers are more powerful when they are large relative to your business or when the purchases represent a high proportion of their costs, as this improves their ability and need to bargain.
   How much of this is relevant to your business? Would any of your customers be interested in integrating backwards and buying either you or one of your competitors? What could be the impact of that happening?

3. *Suppliers:* Relative size is also a source of power here. Suppliers are powerful when there are only a few of them serving an industry and there are few substitutes. They can then raise prices, reduce quality or tighten credit terms at will.

    Does this apply to you? Would any of your suppliers be interested in integrating forwards and buying you or your competitors? What would be the impact of that?

4. *Other potential entrants to the market:* New entrants mean more capacity, which usually increases competition. Where barriers to entry are low, competition can become fierce, with competitors regularly entering the market. Who might those entrants be? How likely is their intervention and how would they make it work? Could you increase the barriers to entry to protect yourself and put potential entrants off?

5. *Substitute products or services:* Substitutes are alternative products that perform in a similar manner to your own products or services. They tend to be produced in markets that make high profits and will be marketed more aggressively. As we become more innovative, no product or service can consider itself immune from the threat of substitution.

    What substitute products and services are there that could affect your own market? What could be the impact of this and how might you tackle it?

Other key external factors

The other factors to take into account can be covered using the acronym STEEPLE, which stands for Sociological, Technological, Economic, Environmental, Political, Legal and Ethical. Many of these are inter-related. For example, changes in demographics can lead to political initiatives to regulate the economy which result in new laws.

If a business does not or is unable to respond to serious pressures from around it, then survival can be threatened. Changed buying patterns, new legislation and especially the general state of the economy can alter the rules of the game.

So now consider the following:

Sociological: What are the key sociological and demographic forces that shape your business? These could include people's attitude to 'profit' and attitudes to work. How do these affect you and is there a predictable trend? This could include the impact of an ageing population, a trend of businesses to cut commuting time by allowing their staff to work from home, or a movement towards more part time and self employed workers.

Technological: What are the key technological forces that shape your business? Few companies are immune from considering this. How do these advances affect you? This could include the increased speed and reducing cost of computing power and the Internet.

Economic: What are the key economic forces that shape your business, both domestically and internationally? How do these affect your business? The economy can be viewed on a scale from booming to recessionary and each will have different connotations for business. Levels of inflation and interest rates can also have an effect.

Environmental: What are the areas that governments and people are becoming more aware and concerned about? These could be pollution, waste or health issues. How do these impact the costs of doing business?

Political: What are the key political forces that shape your business? How do these affect you? These might be the increasing complexity of labour laws and other areas of increased regulation such as Health and Safety. Is more competition being encouraged?

Legal: Some sectors are more heavily regulated than others. What are the legal forces at work and what could be changing?

Ethical: What ethical issues appear to be important at the moment? These could include a greater willingness for people to sue or decisions to boycott businesses whose ethics are questionable.

Any business that is too inward looking is liable to stagnate. What has the above analysis revealed about the business environment and climate that affects you?

Customer or client analysis
The next aspect to consider in choosing a business' Intention is the needs of its customers or clients. History is littered with products that looked interesting, but which too few people wanted or needed and therefore did not buy.

This section will seek to identify who your most important customers are and establish what they need that you either provide or do not provide at the moment.

1. Group your customers into broad categories. Identify the top 20% who provide the greatest contribution to profits. These are not necessarily your largest customers, particularly where they can exert buying power over you.
2. What factors affect the purchasing decisions of each group? This could be quality, service, a key relationship or price. Why do these people buy from you and why might they go to your competitors?
3. What feedback have you or your frontline staff had from your customers? What do they value and what needs to be improved?
4. What do your key customers ask you for that you do not provide at the moment?
5. Is there anything that your key customers are likely to ask you for, if only they knew that you could provide it or that they needed it?

It may be that you cannot answer all of these questions as fully as you would like. Possibly the feedback that your staff receive does not get back to you. If so, this will be something that you will want to bear in mind for later in the process. For now, asking some members of staff for information will give you some clues.

Your revised Intention
Put together the information that you have gathered in the previous two steps, and you may now wish to revise your Intention. This is often the case. Whereas the initial Intention

tends to be woolly and vague, your revised Intention should be more focused. If so, write it as clearly as you can.

Remember that the Intention is defined as a goal whereby the business meets the needs of its customers within the context of the marketplace.

As an example, a Nursing Home developed an Intention that was "to keep the quality and environment of the home at such a high level, that potential relatives and patients can feel this in the first 7 minutes of entering the home... and beyond."

This came from realising that the first impression meant everything in the placing of a patient.

Having established the Intention, you are ready for the next step. You have a message that will act as a guide to you, both now and in the near future. Asking which option is likely to lead you closer to your Intention is an important factor in the decision-making process.

While your Intention must remain as flexible as the environment around the business, it is unlikely that further amendment will be needed during this process.

STEP 4:
ISSUE IDENTIFICATION

It is now necessary to cover the last part of the Information Gathering stage and uncover what the key issues are in the business. Then you can finally go to your staff and ask them for input. By the end of this step you should also have identified some ideas to get started with.

If necessary you can do this on your own, but to get the best results you will want to involve as many people as possible. This will certainly include members of the management team, but also staff and customers.

There is a seven part method for collecting this information. The first three are quite general:
1. Look for clues in your financial accounts.
2. Generally observe what is going on in the business at the moment.
3. Get as many people in the business as possible to complete a general survey.

After reviewing this information, the next four parts will be more focused and will be influenced by the results from the initial review:

4. Interview some of the staff in more detail.
5. Telephone some of your customers or collect them together in a focus group.
6. Observe areas where particular issues have been raised.
7. Map out processes and systems that are causing concern.

There may be no need to cover all of these last four. At the end, all the information needs to be collected and rationalised so that it can be prioritised. This makes it important to keep detailed notes whatever you are doing.

Starting with the general parts:

Part 1 - Financial accounts

Your financial accounts will give you some initial clues as to places to look. Consider the trend of the results over the last few months or years. Probably the most important ratio is that of Return on Equity (for companies) or Return on Capital (for unincorporated bodies). These are the ratios of profitability to owners' funds in the business. As a minimum, this ought to exceed the best savings rate that you can get with a bank. Given the risk involved in investing in a business the return should be a lot higher.

If you need to look in more detail, the Return on Funds ratio can be broken down into three areas:

- The ratio of profit after all costs to sales – the margin
- The ratio of sales to total assets – productivity
- The ratio of assets to owners' funds – leverage

If any of these trends is downwards then you should drill down into more detail. If the net margin is falling, is it the costs that vary with each sale that are rising (variable costs) or the fixed costs that are there irrespective of whether a sale is made? If the productivity ratio is falling, is this because sales are falling or because stock or debtors are increasing?

Of even more use would be to compare your results against those of competitors in a benchmarking exercise. There are various agencies that can provide this type of information, including trade associations.

This information will not, however, give you the whole story. The problem with your accounts is that they will give you the results of what has happened, but they are the result of a great many individual actions. To get closer to that you will need to involve other people.

Part 2 – General observation
First impressions count for a lot in business and in life. If you have a place of business where staff work or customers visit then clues can be found just by trying to look through their eyes at what they see each time they enter. This is easier said than done if you have been there for some time.

Start outside the building and put yourself in the shoes of a prospective customer or employee. The first thing to do is to rate the 'Initial Impressions'. On a scale from 1 (poor) to 7 (excellent), give ratings to:

- The general appearance of the building from the outside;
- The standard of welcome both outside and inside;
- The neatness of reception; and
- The standard of customer care that is displayed.

If you have a factory or production and storage area, use the same scale to rate:
- The general appearance of the production area and its layout;
- The organisation of stock and any work in progress;
- The diligence of workers;
- The interaction and co-operation between workers;
- The age and use of equipment; and
- The evidence of work supervision.

If you have offices, use the same scale to rate:
- The general appearance of the offices and its layout;
- The adequacy of tidiness of storage space;
- The diligence of staff; and
- The standard of office equipment.

Finally, think about any comments of people who have recently visited for the first time. Were they complimentary and, if not, why might that be?

Part 3 – Staff survey
This should be scheduled to happen at the most convenient time. You can choose to present the survey to everyone in the business or select a sample. Covering everyone is normally the better option. It means that everyone gets an opportunity to add to the identification process and have his or her say. Sometimes, however, this is not possible. You may not be able

to get everyone together at the same time. If you are choosing a sample, it needs to be as representative as possible. You can do this by grade, by division or by activity (sales/production etc). Key management should certainly be included, as should the people who know most about what is going on in the business. These must include staff who have customer contact, especially the receptionist!

So far as the design of the survey is concerned, it needs to be as simple as possible, asking questions in a general way that most people will have an answer for.

The following survey is divided into a number of sections so that you can gain a picture of the organisation. The model for the survey is the 'Business Triangle', which suggests that for an organisation to be successful it needs to be strong in three key areas:

1. Management
2. Products & Services
3. Finance

The questions are designed to be general ones that will apply to just about every organisation, but feel free to change them to statements that are more relevant to your organisation. Each statement should be scored between 1 (where there is total disagreement that the statement applies to the business) and 7 (where there is full agreement that the statement applies to the business). There will be some statements when people will not have sufficient knowledge to have an opinion. These should be left blank.

MANAGEMENT

	1 – 7 or n/a
The Vision	
We have a written Business Plan which has been updated in the past year	
Management and staff are clear about the future direction of the business	
There is no resistance to change in the organisation	
Performance is measured regularly and feedback is given	
Staff are encouraged to ask questions and give opinions to management	

The People

We offer flexible contracts to suit the organisation	
Staff are appropriately trained	
The disruption caused by absence is minimal	
Pay is related to performance	
Staff are asked for good ideas and are rewarded for them	

The Systems

The business makes proper use of systems to reduce time and effort	
We set and monitor budgets	
The key ratios of the business are tracked	
Staff are kept informed of matters that affect them	
We comply with all Regulations that are relevant to us	

PRODUCTS & SERVICES

The Selling Process	1 – 7 or n/a
Everyone is involved with the marketing of the business	
We look after existing profitable customers and clients	
We are profit driven and not sales motivated	
We monitor enquiries and conversion rates	
We actively seek feedback from customers and clients	

The Buying Process

Our regular suppliers help us to reduce costs	
Purchasing needs are planned ahead	
Major costs are put out to tender regularly	
We reduce the size of orders unless there is a bulk discount	
The quality and accuracy of goods received are always checked	

The Production Process

All work is planned to be completed quickly and effectively	
We have removed any part of the process where no value is added	
Work moves through the operation with no delay	
Storage space is utilised effectively/files are easily retrieved	
Delivery routes are planned and efficient	

FINANCE

Operating Assets	1 – 7 or n/a
There is no wasted room in our buildings	
We have no obsolete stock or work in progress	
Invoicing takes place as soon as possible after the sale	
Debt collection practices are applied rigorously	
Supplier invoices are paid when they are due	

Overheads and Taxation

Staff are encouraged to find ways of reducing overheads	
Travel and entertainment costs are tightly controlled	
Our insurance broker gets the best deal for us	
We have a tax planning session before the end of the year	
The tax bill is minimised by efficiently extracting profits	

Cash and Funding

Rolling cash flow forecasts are prepared	
We are honest about funding problems that arise	
The structure of funding matches the assets	
Keyman cover is in place to protect the value of the business	
We monitor bank balances regularly	

It is essential that everyone knows that the replies will be confidential and that none of the statements will be attributed. If you suspect that this may be a problem and that people will not give their honest opinions, then bring in someone independent to process the returned forms for you.

So plan to do this as soon as possible. Ideally you should get them all together, or do this in groups if there are too many. To get the best response you will need to explain:

- Why the survey is being done and where it fits into the Profit Improvement Project
- The incentives that you agreed for everyone who takes part
- That the replies will be confidential and no comments will be attributed to individuals
- That they can therefore be as honest as possible
- That they should focus on the whole organisation rather than their individual department or division
- That they should complete the survey and return it immediately

If it is not possible to get everyone together, you can send it to everyone, but with the above points in the message.

Getting the surveys back as soon as possible means that the results of the first three parts of the survey can then be averaged, excluding 'not applicable' scores. By running the scores for each section through a 'Radar' chart, you will be able to analyse your organisation in the three key areas against the perfect 7 score. It should look something like this:

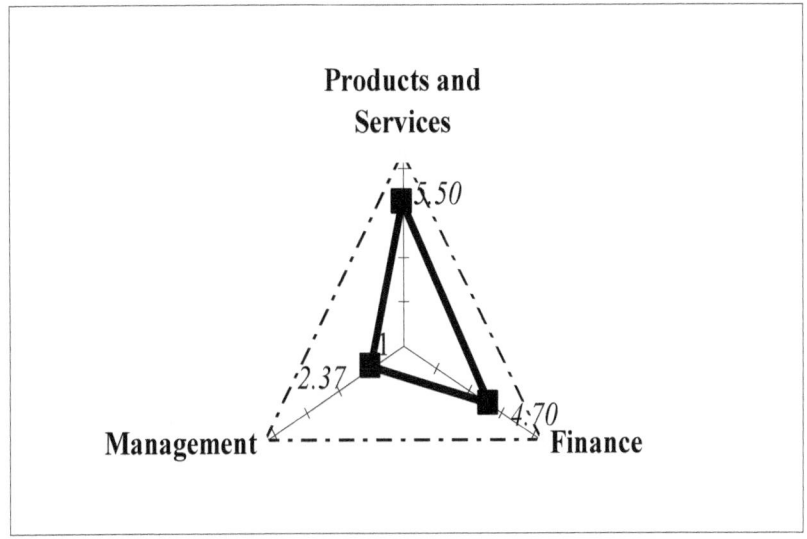

In this example it can be seen that the Management part is the weakest. In fact, if this organisation gets much weaker in that area then the triangle could be ready to fall over. Wherever the weakest areas are, identify the statements that have caused this. You will need to look beyond the simple averages. For example, any statement where 50% or more of the respondents scored 3 or less is also an area of weakness. Any statement where more than 30% scored 2 or less is clearly an area of concern. These are clues as to the problems that could be holding back the profitability of the business.

At the end of this section you should have a list of general issues that have been collected together from the work to date. It is unlikely, however, that you will know the full reasons behind them. These areas now need to be looked at in more detail through the following techniques.

Part 4 – Staff interviews

The results of the survey will give you more information than just looking at the accounts, but you will need to dig deeper to get the best from the exercise. Interviewing just a few of the staff, and asking the right questions, will produce a flood of useful information.

As the staff answered the survey anonymously, you will have to select those to be interviewed in more detail based on your knowledge of them. Who are the more positive members of the team? Who are the ones who have had good ideas before?

Invite them individually into a quiet room and start by re-emphasizing the purpose of the exercise and the importance of their honesty. Start by asking some of these general questions:

- What is your understanding of the direction that the organisation is heading in?
- How could customer satisfaction be improved?
- What upsets the customers so much that they consider leaving?
- How is staff morale and how do you think it could be improved?
- Where are staff most stretched?
- What is the one thing that has brought you closest to leaving?
- Is everyone adequately trained? Where is the greatest need?
- Where are the bottlenecks in our processes?
- How could the quality of work be improved?
- If you were in charge, what three changes would you make?

After these general questions have been answered, you will then be able to see if they can explain what is behind some of the other general issues that have arisen so far. You should allow an hour for each interview and none should last more than 90 minutes. This will give you enough time to find out what you need to, but not too much that the session drags on.

The interviews should ideally be either side of lunch. You will need the break to absorb the issues that arose in the morning.

Part 5 – Customer interviews or focus groups
It would also be helpful to interview maybe four of your key customers over the phone. These calls should take no more than 20 minutes each. Alternatively, arrange for a number of them to visit and form a focus group.

Explain the purpose of the call or the meeting and encourage them to be as honest as possible. They should be pleased to help you if it means that you are trying to improve customer service! If you are meeting them, this would be a good opportunity to treat them to a meal afterwards as a "thank you".

The following general questions will warm things up:

- How easy is it to do business with us?
- What would improve the business relationship?
- Why do you choose to do business with us rather than the competition?
- How would you rate the sales people that you work with?
- How would you rate the operations people that you deal with?
- What percentage of the time do we get it right first time?
- How responsive are we to fixing problems?
- How is our administration?
- What would cause you to do more business with us?

Should any issues arise from a question, dig further to get to the real issues and then raise general issues that you have discovered which impact on the customer.

Part 6 – Observe specific areas

If there was a specific area of the business that was identified as being a problem area, a better alternative to interviewing the staff who work there is to go to that area. A combination of watching what is happening and asking questions of the staff as work is carried on should uncover the reasons for the problems that have been identified.

Part 7 – Review systems and processes

If a problem cannot be pinned down to one part of a business, it may be necessary to map out an entire system or process to spot the cause of the problem and identify the reasons.

Take the example of a factory that manufactures widgets. These go through a number of processes from raw material to finished product. Along the way, the parts need to be transported from one operation to another and inspected. Inevitably there can be some delay along the way. However, the business boasts that it holds stocks that average only 4 days of raw materials and 2 days of finished goods and the factory operates for 8 hours per day. It has been found that the procedure is as follows:

- The raw materials are taken from the store 32 hours after they are delivered. It takes 15 minutes for the storekeeper to select the materials and 20 minutes to take these parts to the start of the production line.

- The first parts are assembled in 70 minutes; there is then a 5 minute journey to the next part of the line.

- There is a hold-up of 8 minutes before fitting takes place (fitting takes 25 minutes).

- There is a 3 minute journey to the testing area where the queue is normally 6 hours.

- It takes 1 minute to test the widget before going to finished stock.

Process Map

PRODUCT: *Widget*

DATE:

MAPPER:

No	Step Description	Time (mins)	Operation (O)	Transport (T)	Inspect (I)	Store (S)	Delay (D)
1	Raw material	1920				*	
2	Parts select	15			*		
3	Transport to line	20		*			
4	Assembly	70	*				
5	Transport	5		*			
6	Hold-up	8					*
7	Fitting	25	*				
8	Transport to testing	3		*			
9	Queue	360					*
10	Testing	1			*		
11	Finished stock	960				*	
	Total	3387					
	Operations	95					
	Percentage Operations	2.8%					

When the process is looked at in this way, it becomes easier to see how and where changes need to be made. During anything other than an 'operation', no value is being added and 'waste' of some description is taking place.

Collect and rationalise the information
Your notes may now be quite confusing, with lots of information covered. In order to bring some order to your notes, it is wise to go through each point individually and transfer them into a more logical order.

Mindmap - One alternative is to use a number of Mindmap diagrams, which will give a visual view of the issues. This involves taking a separate piece of paper for each of the nine sections of the Business Triangle, e.g. The Vision, The People etc. Put these headings in the centre of each page and transfer your main issues onto the page that most closely fits. This will be connected as branches to the main heading. Other issues may then become smaller branches.

Affinity diagram - Otherwise, write all the points that you find on a stack of sticky notes and then arrange them into related groups. After you have grouped the notes, develop a title or heading. The heading should be short and describe the main theme of the group that it represents. Now look for relationships between them that may mean that groups need to be combined.

Find and prioritise the key issues

Review each point that you have come up with, no matter how small. Some of the points will have clustered with others to become more significant.

Bear in mind the '7 Golden Questions of Profit Improvement':

1. Where could staff become more involved in the planning and running of the business?
2. How can more of the better customers be retained?
3. How can you sell more to existing customers?
4. Where are the opportunities to sell to more customers?
5. Where is the waste in the process?
6. How could the organisation's systems be improved?
7. Where is the conflict between departments?

There should be two main areas that you have identified:

- Issues where solutions have presented themselves during the day, which are worthy of further consideration
- Issues that are clearly important and holding the organisation back, but which have not yet been resolved

The solutions that are worthy of further consideration will be considered first thing tomorrow. You should exclude, however, anything that could not be solved in a group context, or which is personal. These need to be solved separately. Ideally you should be left with no more than 7 major unsolved issues. Should you have more than this number, some further rationalisation will be necessary. Some of them will have to be targeted at a later date. Which are the ones that you believe to be most urgent in needing to be rectified? In particular, which ones are holding the organisation back from reaching the destination identified earlier?

Martin Leith's I-Scan

Indications

What are the signs that action is required? A key question is this: If, while you were sleeping tonight, a miracle were to occur and the problem were to clear up instantly, how would you know when you woke up that the miracle had happened?

Influences

What are the contributing factors and antecedents?

Implications

What are the likely consequences? What benefits are gained as a by-product of the problem remaining unsolved?

Interests

Who has an interest in things changing? Who has an interest in things staying the same? Who will be affected to a greater or lesser extent by the change? Who is the owner of the problem or the initiator of the change programme? Who else is involved?

Impulses

What might help the innovation or change process?

Impediments

What might impede, inhibit or hinder the innovation or change process?

Inter-related issues

How does the issue under consideration connect with other issues? What is the problem costing? Consider actual cost and opportunity cost, past and future. Also consider non-monetary costs: time, emotional energy, etc.

Inconsistencies

What are the exceptions to the problem pattern? What conditions are present when the problem **does not** happen?

Inefficacies

What has been tried that has not worked? What do these attempts have in common? Is there a pattern?

Injunctions

What are the givens, the positive and negative specifications, the parameters, the musts and must nots? What is non-negotiable?

Intuitions

Do you have any hunches or gut feelings about this project?

Inventory

What resources and capabilities do you have at your disposal? What resources and capabilities are missing?

+ Time	+ Money
+ People	+ Skills
+ Support	+ Specialist knowledge
+ Information	+ Equipment
+ Accommodation	+ Other resources (specify)

When you are down to no more than 7 issues, gather together the details of all of them. A useful structure to use is the 'I-Scan' which is summarised on the previous page. This is an Information Gathering tool, but it can sometimes help problems to dissolve without further effort. Some of the 12 sections may not be relevant.

Sorting the Issues

With the fuller understanding of what each issue represents, are any of them connected? Having established the connections between issues, what comes first and could be causing others? After putting these all together in a diagram, it can often be found that just one or two key issues are at the root of many others. These need to be identified and confronted tomorrow, not avoided.

Conclusion

At the end of this day, collect together the results of the accounts review and survey, the ideas and solutions that you want to consider further in Step 6, which is the Implementation step, and the details of the issues that you want to be resolved as soon as possible.

The Information Gathering part of the exercise is now complete.

STEP 5:
IDEA GENERATION

You may have thought that going through the Information Gathering stages alone would have been sufficient to generate plenty of ideas. While you will have collected some ideas already, experience suggests that these are merely scratching the surface of what is possible.

To date you are likely to have collected only the more obvious ideas that are unlikely to address the key issues that the business faces. Having decided what the key issues are at the present time, there is a need to have a special event to tackle them. Getting your key staff together to focus on these key issues will be the object of the day.

Planning the day
For a start, the day needs a title. Calling it a 'Profit Improvement Day' does not work for everyone. An 'Improvement Day' is better; the choice is up to you -what will work best in your business?

The next thing to decide is who from the business should be involved in the day. It was said earlier that the secret of successful Profit Improvement is to use *everyone's* ideas and abilities to the greatest advantage.

People who you may have interviewed already should certainly be there. They will probably have had some additional thoughts since the interview and be willing to share them. In addition, look for people who are:

- Informed – the people who know what is going on in the business
- Integral – the key individuals in the business
- Interested – only people who want to be there should attend
- Incisive – people who get straight to the point
- Inquiring – people who ask questions
- Inventive – the creative people who will have some solutions

When considering how many people to involve, remember that out of every 7 to 10 people, one of them needs to be happy to be a group leader.

The agenda of the day should be split into 7 sessions:

1. Introduction to the day (10 mins)
2. Intentions of the business (15 mins)
3. Information gathering results (30 mins) followed by a break
4. Ideas workshop session
5. Interval for lunch
6. Issues workshop session
7. Ideas Plan review from the different groups (20 mins)

From this it can be seen that the day starts 'global', before going 'local' and reverting back to 'global' again.

The invitation to the day should explain what is planned in detail. A copy of the agenda should therefore be attached, along with a list of the key issues that the organisation faces. Staff need to be aware that they will be asked to identify the 7 'i's of the solution and therefore:

- Consider the issues that the business is facing and **Identify** a wide range of **Ideas**
- Gain consensus as a group and decide whether these ideas should be **Implemented**
- Agree the **Individual** responsible for implementing the idea, its **Impact** on the business, **Input** required and the **Increase** in Profits that would result from successful Implementation

By giving them notice of these things prior to the session, staff have a chance to think about the possible solutions.

The venue for the workshop should, if possible, be away from the business. This is desirable as it reduces the chance that anyone will be disturbed during the day and makes it easier for people to focus on what can possibly be achieved rather than feeling restricted.

When selecting and setting a meeting room:

- Look for one with little or no outside noise and as much natural light as possible
- Tables and chairs need to be arranged in a horse-shoe shape with space in between
- Allow tea, coffee, soft drinks and fruit to be available all the time

At a more detailed level:

- You may need to borrow or hire a computer projector and screen to present the results of the survey and the final plan
- There needs to be a flipchart and pens for each group
- Each attendee should be provided with paper and pens for notes
- There should be place cards for each person, particularly where some of the delegates are not well known to each other
- Make sure you have plenty of your chosen Incentives, e.g. the cash or vouchers, ready. Three or four for each person should be allowed for
- Each group leader needs a number of copies of the blank Ideas Plan to record the ideas (an example will be presented later)

On the day itself
You and the other organisers will need to arrive early to ensure that all the arrangements have been made correctly and to be available to welcome attendees as they arrive. It is helpful if a pack is presented to each attendee on arrival that includes:

- The workshop objectives
- The agenda
- A summary of the key issues identified
- The groups and their leaders if there are more than 10 attendees
- The rules of the workshop sessions
- A 'Seven Ideas to Improve Performance and Profitability' form
- Implementation worksheets

The groups should be mixed. It is preferable if the people have not worked together before.

The three initial presentations in the agenda are essential in order to set the scene and warm people up, but they should not overrun.

Introduction – session 1
The short introduction should explain the structure and objectives of the day. It should cover a summary of the process that is being worked through. The position and importance of this process should be explained.

Intentions of the business – session 2
The presentation by the owner or Chief Executive should explain the Intention of the business that was decided in Step

3, as this will give a focus to the proceedings. The emphasis should be on honesty and candour, demonstrating that the business has faced reality. If there is time, allow people to comment.

Information Gathering – session 3
The presentation continues the scene setting and should cover:

- the highs and lows of the staff survey
- a radar diagram showing the Business Triangle
- a summary of the ideas that came from the survey and interviews that you believe should be implemented
- a list of the key issues that remain

The presentation might also cover a summary of the trading position of the organisation, unless this is common knowledge. Many of the delegates are unlikely to have much idea about the financial stability of the organisation. It can only help to put things in perspective.

A couple of slides that show the profit and loss account and balance sheet, with an explanation of what the numbers mean, can be very useful in helping people to understand how the business is doing and how it may need their help. The more information that can be given, the better it is. Go back to the work that you did at the start of the last step when looking at the financial accounts of the business. Is there information here that could be shown to everyone?

If you were able to get any information on competitors it would be useful to show some of this as well, identifying where they seem to be ahead of you.

Ideas workshop – session 4

The two sessions either side of the lunch interval will form the main part of the day. What has gone before has been important preparation and before the delegates break up into their groups one final piece of preparation is needed.

Everyone should be asked the question:

> "If we are successful in identifying additional profits today, how would you like to see it used?"

The answers that generally come back are varied but are likely to include things like:

- Higher pay, benefits or dividends
- Investment in new equipment or marketing and sales effort
- Reduction of debt
- The ability to recruit specialist staff
- Buying other businesses

At this particular point in the process, the question is key. Allowing many people to have their say now means that they can see that there is something in the results for them.

It was said that there needs to be a leader or facilitator for each group of 7 to 10 delegates. The most important thing that the facilitators have to bear in mind is that their role is not to deliver ideas and solutions but to serve their group. After introducing themselves and making sure that everyone knows each other, the first job of the facilitator is to lay out the ground rules. This is best done by explaining the WORKSHOP RULES which are in two parts and are found on the following page.

For delegates:

Work together as a team - *the results will always be better than if you all work as individuals.*

One person to talk at a time – *if more than one person is talking, then someone is not listening.*

Respect each other's opinions – *it is dangerous to scoff at other people.*

Keep an open mind about everything – *closed minds can lead to a closed business.*

Speak up and say what needs to be said – withhold nothing – *it is only by speaking up that the best ideas get heard.*

Help the group to use its time effectively – be concise – *time will be short and will fly during the sessions.*

Only discuss key issues – avoid side-tracks and tangents – *with limited time available, people need to keep to the point.*

Personal attacks and sarcasm are unhelpful – *they are banned.*

The facilitators will:

Record the key decisions taken – *by writing down the actions and calling them back, everyone will be clear about what has been agreed.*

Unleash the power of the group – *encourage them to work together.*

Let the discussion flow, but keep focused on the key issues.

Encourage everyone to have his or her say – *sometimes the quietest people have the best thoughts to offer.*

Serve the group in a neutral capacity and call foul if rules are broken – *you can call foul by rustling paper.*

The first part explains what delegates are to do and the second covers the objectives of the facilitator.

It can be seen that the skilful facilitator will be able to:

- Be a neutral servant to the group and focus its energy
- Be more concerned about the process of the session rather than the content
- Help the group to make the greatest progress by abiding by the rules
- Swiftly move items not on the agenda or not agreed onto another meeting

The skilful facilitator will also be able to 'read' the group by watching the body language and reactions of individuals. They need to be attentive to whoever is speaking at the time while watching for others that may want to contribute. The skilful facilitator will also be able to manage their own body language by, for example:

- Using a voice that encourages participation
- Knowing when to pause and use silence
- Standing or sitting back from the table if more authority is required

These are particularly important at the start of any session, especially in a group that has not worked together before and needs to get used to one another before they discuss the key issues. For this reason the first session should start with some form of open discussion to get things moving in the right direction.

Either ask everyone "How would you like to see the organisation in seven years?", or alternatively, consider using some of the following:

- What makes this organisation successful?
- What are our strengths and weaknesses?
- What are the opportunities and threats that we face?
- If you could change one thing in the organisation, what would it be?

Especially in the opening period, the facilitator should ask open questions such as "What do you think about....?"; "What is your opinion of....?"; "If Mark thinks that we should...then what do you think?" Closed questions should only be used when the facilitator is trying to close and end a discussion of a particular point. For example, "Do you agree that.....?" Comments and questions should be redirected between individuals to give others the opportunity to voice their opinion and if a comment needs to be clarified then the facilitator can paraphrase for understanding and clarity.

The 'Five Whys' technique can be useful in getting down to the bones of a problem. Using this, the question to each answer given is 'Why?' However, watch for defensive responses.

Even at this early stage it will be clear that there are a number of 'difficult participants', who for various reasons are ignoring the rules. The most common ones are:

Talkative Tim/Tina – he or she may be well informed, but could be eager to show off knowledge. A reminder of the need to be concise could be along the lines of "That is interesting – what do others think?"

Arguing Alan/Alice – they may have a combative personality or be upset by an individual point. Either find something that they say that you can genuinely agree with and move onto something else, or toss an obviously incorrect remark to the group. As a last resort take them to one side during the next break.

Rambling Rob/Rose – easily strays from the issue being discussed and cannot find a way back, so carries on! When they pause for breath, thank them, restate the relevant key issues and say "We really need to get back to the subject" before moving on.

Silent Simon/Simone – they are probably shy by nature or lacking in confidence. Rather than asking them directly, ask the opinion of the person next to them and then move onto them. These people tend to be listening and tend to have something important to say if given the opportunity.

When the facilitator believes that the group is 'warmed up' with everyone having contributed to the discussion, everyone can turn to the 'Seven Ideas to Improve Performance and Profitability' form, which should have 7 boxes on one page that look like this:

Idea:	Initials:

Issue that this Idea will solve:

Everyone should complete just the first box with their best idea and fill in their initials, then pass the form to their left. Having received a new form, the second idea can be one that they already had in mind, or another idea that could have been inspired by what their neighbour wrote.

If someone gets stuck, they pass the form on and wait to receive the next one from their right. Seeing what others have written is often inspiring. The process continues until as many boxes as possible have been completed. It is generally found that the last few ideas, while being the most difficult to get out, may be the best!

The next step is to collect the ideas and take an inventory. If you have 10 people in a group and each paper has 7 ideas, there could be up to 70 ideas to consider. Therefore the ideas need to be broken down into groups and it has been found that doing this by ease of implementation works well.

This means that you now need 3 pieces of flipchart paper for each group. These can be headed up:
- 'Indisputably easy'
- 'In-betweens' and
- 'Immensely difficult'

Having returned the sheets to whoever wrote the first idea on it, start by asking everyone for the idea on his or her sheet that would be the easiest to implement. This will be the one which, if agreed, could even be put into practice tomorrow. Your description on the 'Indisputably easy' flipchart should take up no more than one line. Include the initials of the person whose idea it was.

People may say things in this section that the facilitator thinks will be far from easy and extremely complicated, but the temptation to say this must be resisted. If anything, try to greet each idea with a positive comment such as "Yes, we might try that" or "That's an interesting thought, we should look at that at some point." Also to be resisted is any detailed discussion at this stage. If the idea has real merit then there will be time for consideration later.

The second stage is to ask everyone for the idea on their sheet that would be the hardest to implement and record these in the same way on the 'Immensely difficult' flipchart. That will leave you to collect ideas that people have left that have not been covered already. These can either go on the 'In-between' flipchart or the person can nominate one of the other flipcharts to put it on.

After everyone is happy that the ideas that they would like to have discussed are somewhere on the flipcharts, go to the 'Indisputably easy' chart and let the group choose the one that they would like to discuss in detail first.

With the group having agreed the easiest one to start with, the person whose idea it was in the first place should explain it in some more detail to the group. The facilitator should then let the discussion flow with the WORKSHOP RULES in the background, being used only when necessary.

Each idea should be discussed in 3 steps, with people giving their opinions of why the idea is 1) Ingenious, and 2) Inadequate, before agreeing how it can be 3) Improved.

Be aware that no matter how simple and straightforward the idea may seem, this first idea is usually the most difficult to get agreed.

Everyone needs to have his or her say, no matter how brief. When you believe that everyone has reached a consensus, ask for the idea to be captured. This should follow the example on the following page.

IDEAS PLAN

Idea No	Idea description	Idea contributor	Impact 1= High 7= Low	Input required 1= Low 7 High	Impl'n Date	Individual responsible	Increase in profits	Comments
1.								
2.								
3.								

Adapted from 'All About Earnings', Schimel & Kravitz

- *Idea description* should describe the initiative that is going to make the business more profitable. This should be done in bullet point form to capture the essence of the idea rather than the detail.

- *Idea contributor* is the person who wrote the idea on the list. This person should be rewarded with one of your chosen Incentives at this point. The first time that this happens often has a remarkable effect on the group.

- *Impact* on the business should be graded on a scale of 1 to 7 with a '1' being given to a high impact while '7' is given to one of low importance.

- *Input required* should also be graded between 1 and 7 with a '1' being given where there is little input required while '7' is given to the most difficult ones.

- *Implementation date* is the date when it is planned that the idea will be put into practice and earning additional revenues or profit.

- *Individual responsible* is the one person from the group who volunteers to take the idea on when the day is ended and makes sure that it gets implemented. It does not have to be the most senior person in the group who takes this on. Often the person whose ideas it was in the first place will feel strongly enough about it to make sure that the idea does not go to waste. This person should also be rewarded with one of the Incentives. No matter how straightforward the idea may seem, implementation is rarely easy!

- *Increase in profits* – this is often the final test for an idea. If the group cannot demonstrate through some simple assumptions that the idea is going to improve performance and profitability, then should time be taken up with implementing it? If this proves difficult, then serious consideration should be given to leaving the idea to one side and moving onto something else.

People can get carried away with the positive emotions of the session and have wildly inflated views of the impact of the ideas. The facilitator's job is always to test the assumptions and, if there is any doubt as to the prudence of the estimates, they should offer to halve or even quarter the assumptions 'just to be on the safe side'.

Unrealistically high targets are as de-motivating as low or non-existent targets.

When each idea has been captured in this form, the facilitator needs to make it clear that the discussion on the subject is closed and it is time to move onto another idea. This can be done by clearly crossing it from the flipchart and rewarding the 'Idea contributor' and 'Individual responsible'. Each time, he or she should allow the group to decide which of the remaining ideas is to be discussed next. The first two or three ideas should come from the 'Indisputably easy' list.

When the facilitator is satisfied that the process is running smoothly, then the other two flipcharts can be opened up for consideration.

If other ideas come up which are in a related area, take care not to get diverted. These ideas should be captured in an 'Ideas bin' for consideration later.

Before the interval for lunch it is useful to summarise the ideas that have been captured during the session. Delegates should be asked to consider the remaining list and think about the ones that they really want to cover at some point in the next session. Ask for their feedback on the morning session.

Interval for lunch workshop – session 5
During the interval, where there have been a number of groups at work, the group leaders should:

- Spend some time together to discuss how they found the Ideas workshop session and reveal what has been agreed. It is surprisingly rare that two groups will have been discussing exactly the same idea, but sometimes they will have attempted a solution of the same problem from different but complementary directions;
- Discuss which issues definitely need to be covered in the next session, especially those key issues that were identified already as driving many others. No two groups should talk through the same solutions this afternoon;
- Be available to take comments from team members that they might not have wanted aired in the session; and
- If possible, record the plans to date on one combined set.

Issues workshop – session 6

The afternoon session will have a slightly different format. Groups are now given a short-list of the issues that have not been addressed already and are able to choose one only.

Each group discusses its particular issue. The first approach is known as 'Imagineering'. The group is asked to describe a time in the future when the issue has been solved and there are no problems of any kind. From this description they are asked to work backwards and describe the steps that were necessary to achieve this. When this has gone as far as it can, they can then work forwards 'Incrementally' from where they are now and describe each step that needs to be taken. This will not necessarily lead to the same place that they started from.

Should this process falter, encourage some way out or odd ideas. Think of the 'Impossible' and ask "Wouldn't it be wonderful if...?"

Even though the issues being discussed are likely to be harder than those covered in the morning, the afternoon session is often easier and flows better as the clock ticks on.

Before breaking again, summarise the extra progress made to the group and clear any final issues that may be there.

Ideas Plan review – session 7

After the break, get all the groups back together. Each facilitator should present the ideas from their group to everyone. If these can be displayed on a screen for everyone to see that would be an advantage. This will explain in outline the ideas agreed to be taken forward. Remember to include the ideas that came out from yesterday's survey and interviews.

The conclusion session
During the concluding sessions, thank everyone for their contribution during the day and explain the next steps. In outline the next steps will be that:

- Early tomorrow all of the ideas are to be considered and prioritised by a small team.
- An overall plan will be produced that will be circulated to everyone and a number of people will be contacted to agree how these high priority ideas are to be progressed as soon as possible.

It is worth explaining to everyone at this point that it is most unlikely that all of the ideas will be able to go ahead straight away. To do this risks the organisation suffering from 'Initiative overload' and important operational work being left.

The final task is to ask everyone to complete the following sentence:

"I intend to support this Improvement Process by............."

Get as many people as possible to read out what they have written. This reinforces their commitment to follow through later.

When the day is over

Now you can turn your attention to those issues that could not be raised today. Do any of the initiatives on the Ideas Plan to date address these? If not, what actions now need to be taken? This can sometimes be established by going through the stages of the process for each problem. Therefore, write out for each one:

1) *Introduction* to the problem.
2) *Incentives* for solving the problem. Where is the pain to be avoided and where are the gains to be made?
3) *Intention*. Where do you hope to get to?
4) *Issues*. What are they?
5) *Ideas*. List up to 7 options and then comment on them before choosing one or a combination.

Include your chosen solution on the Ideas Plan in the same format, although these may need to be ones that you yourself are responsible for.

But we can't afford to take a day to do this!

This is a familiar cry at the suggestion that the organisation takes a day away from the business. Many people believe that they are indispensable and are then amazed when the organisation functions quite well without them when they take a holiday or are sick. Sometime, however, it really is not possible to take too many people away for an entire day. This does not mean that there is no chance of making something of the opportunity.

One solution is to break the full day down into a series of 2 hour sessions, with the following format:

Session one: the general introductions and the collection of the inventory of ideas.

Session two: start with the 'Indisputably easy' ideas only. Have a full discussion and plan them.

Session three and subsequent sessions: start by reviewing the progress of the implementation of the ideas agreed in the previous session, before carrying on with the inventory of ideas and eventually tackling the tough remaining issues.

The benefit of this particular approach is clear. As everyone knows when the next session is, and that implementation is the first item on the agenda, implementation is more likely to happen!

STEP 6:
IMPLEMENTING THE PLANS

Great ideas are meaningless and worthless unless they are successfully implemented, and it is common for additional profits not to be realised because of a breakdown in the implementation process. Anyone who has played sports such as football, tennis or golf will know that the power in a shot comes not from hitting the ball, but from the follow through. And so it is with Profit Improvement.

This is the final part of the Information Gathering, Idea Generation and Implementation Guidance cycle. While in previous steps we have tried to make the first two stages as complete as possible so that the best ideas have been planned at this stage, it is the work from today that really determines the success of the project. For various reasons businesses find that putting ideas into operation is never easy. This is why it was recommended that existing initiatives be rationalised in Step 1. If you have followed the process through, you will now have plenty of initiatives to add to the list!

Why is implementation so difficult?
The answers to this question are many and varied. We have
moved from the rational gathering and analysis of information
and facts to implementation. This is now about people, and
people are not fully rational. It is understood that, as a race,
humans are most comfortable when things stay the same. In
fact we actively resist change wherever feasible.

Many of us enjoy studying a situation and analysing it. We
then talk a lot about change and plan the necessary actions.
Yet we do not always get beyond the talking stage. We stay in
our comfort zone and avoid the hard work that change
requires. In fact, when anything out of the ordinary happens,
if anything 'changes', there starts an emotional roller coaster,
whether we like it or not. This applies whether we are
proposing to put a new sign over the photocopier telling
people what to do when it goes wrong, to the introduction of A
new computer system that will monitor the work that
everyone is doing.

The journey has been described in many ways, one of which is
the DREAD of change:

- Denial
- Resistance
- Exploration
- Acceptance
- Doing it

The goal of implementation is to get all parties through the
cycle as quickly and painlessly as possible.

Is there a solution?
Probably the biggest problem with implementation is that
people think that having followed a process such as this, they
should now be able to just take each idea, go ahead and
implement or 'do it'. In fact, in all but the simplest example,
this leads straight to difficulties and trouble. Pushing ahead
too fast does not give enough time for those who are going
through the DREAD cycle.

Think back to your preparation in Step 1. You had the idea to
improve profitability of the business. Could you just go ahead
and 'do it'? We have seen that to be successful, there is a
process that needs to be followed, in an order that is important.
Here, 6 steps later, you are in a similar position. You have
ideas that you want to do something with but without a
process to follow in a certain order, too much is left to chance.
The following process has been designed to avoid such
problems and the stages should be familiar to you as *they
mirror the steps that have been taken to get this far!* This means
that for each individual idea, there could be a need to:

- Make it clear what the **Incentives** are
- Describe and review the **Intention** of the idea – what is it to
  achieve?
- Identify **Issues** that will help or hinder implementation,
  and address the latter, such as questions of resources and
  skills
- Generate **Ideas** to construct the detailed plan that is now
  required

If any of these is missing, success becomes less certain. Having
followed that mini process for each idea it will be clear what
needs to be done, and in what order.

Another major problem now faced is rooted in the Law of Diminishing Intent. The further you get away from deciding to do something, the harder it becomes to get started. For this reason, key management of the organisation should get together to discuss the plans that came from the workshops soon afterwards. This might not be a popular meeting to call. People will have been away from the office for the workshop and feel that they have a day's work to catch up on, but everything will lose momentum by not pressing ahead quickly.

The first thing to do is test the continuing validity of the ideas proposed. In the cold light of a new day, back in the real world of the business, each idea needs to be reconsidered in terms of:

- Does it bring the business closer to achieving its Intention?
- Is the idea still valid, having thought about it further?
- Is the value of its impact correct or does this need to be altered? Is the rating of 'input required' correct, or does this need to be revised?
- Is the Implementation date assigned to the idea realistic, or is it likely that more time will be needed to do this properly?
- Is the Increase in profits realistic?
- Has the right individual been nominated to be responsible for the implementation of the idea?
- Most importantly, is there a good chance that the idea can be implemented?

In many cases it may be found that, even with the facilitator testing the assumptions during the workshop sessions, the groups have been too optimistic. While it could be considered

76

dangerous to amend the plans in this way, doing so gives the initiative a greater chance of success than allowing unrealistic assumptions to be perpetuated and inappropriate individuals to continue their involvement.

Bear in mind the key issues that were identified at the start of Step 4. Solutions to the key issues that were identified to the workshop group ought to have the highest importance.

Having discussed each idea, it should be possible to produce a revised overall plan which has assumptions that management are now happy with. Some of the ideas may even have been taken out altogether, but it is better to do it at this stage than to use and waste valuable resources.

The list should now be prioritised. As the saying goes, "To accomplish nothing, attempt everything." To get an initial rough idea of the priorities, multiply the 'Impact' score of each idea with that of the 'Input Required'. The lowest score will be 1 and the highest will be 49, although it will be rare to find any on the list that score that high. The most important ideas, which will take the smallest input to implement, should now be at the top of the list. Anything scoring more than 30 should be discounted immediately.

Starting at the top of the list, allocate a start date to each of the ideas, bearing in mind the resources in terms of time and costs that each idea will take up. The objective is to select some easy winners to get started with. These should be quick to implement rather than important to the organisation, as success in these can give momentum to the more difficult initiatives that are to follow. It may now be necessary to amend the implementation dates one final time. There should certainly be no more than ten initiatives to start now.

If necessary, have two lists. The first will have the top priority actions; the other will contain initiatives that will start next year. This year's plan should now be circulated to everyone who attended the workshop. This will need to be accompanied with some notes explaining why some ideas no longer feature in the plan and why the priorities might have changed. Finally, everyone should be told which ideas are being started first.

The 'Total Implementation Model' can now be started.

Agree the Incentives
Select the top idea and, bearing in mind the estimated profit increase, confirm the incentive linked to successful implementation. Remember that too many initiatives fail because there is no tangible benefit to the people who are managing the work.

Confirm the Intention of the idea
Get together with the person who has taken responsibility for implementation. This person must now be involved in developing the practicalities. They may now have some misgivings about having volunteered to take the task on and will need to be coached if that is the case. You will be armed with a clear commitment from the top of the organisation to support the idea and give the appropriate staff the time to complete the project. If necessary, they will be able to prioritise their existing duties and responsibilities.

In order to build the confidence of the individual responsible, help them to complete the following Intentions worksheet.

Keep in mind that, although the goal may seem miles away, it gets closer only when you take this first step towards it.

INTENTIONS WORKSHEET
Initiative name:
Individual responsible:
Implementation completion date:
Intention description: a)   the initiative goal   b)   the issue solved   c)   the increase in profits estimated
Initiative benefits:
Initiative deliverables:

Identify the detailed issues

This second worksheet can now be completed:

ISSUES IDENTIFICATION WORKSHEET
Initiative name:
Individual responsible:
Implementation completion date:
Influences that might help the initiative, *e.g. frustration with the way things are:*
Influences that might hinder the initiative, *e.g. impact on operations:*
Input that will be required, *e.g. time and cost:*
Individuals who will be able to help:
Important other factors to address:

Generate the detailed ideas and plans

This third part of the worksheet can now be completed in draft. This sheet will be the one that needs to be most flexible. If at all possible collect together the individuals who need to be involved and who have volunteered to help. The same rules as applied at the workshop continue to be useful:

IDEA AND PLAN WORKSHEET				
Initiative name:				
Individual responsible overall:				
Implementation completion date:				
Task number	Description of the task	Resources required	Due date	Individual responsible
010				
020				
030				
040				
050				
060				
070				

Note that the task numbers do not start at 1, which means that tasks that are later identified can be slotted in, or sub-tasks can be inserted under each task.

This is quite a simple worksheet. For more complicated plans where there are a number of interdependencies, it would be recommended that project planning software be used. As with the overall Ideas Plan, this completed plan needs to be communicated. People need to know:

- What is happening?
- Where is it happening?
- Who will be affected?
- Why it is happening?
- How it will happen?
- When it will happen?

Implementation!
The tasks can now be started before the Law of Diminishing Intent starts to kick in. For very simple ideas following the Total Implementation Model might be overkill but, so long as little time is lost in completing the worksheets, this is one case where too much beats too little.

Select the next initiative and go back to step one!

There are no guarantees!
Even following the above system, there is only so much that
anyone can do to be successful in implementing. To some
extent you cannot force staff to do something, even if they
have signed up to it voluntarily. Incentives and sanctions may
help. The best tool that you can ever have is the power of
persuasion.

In the final analysis 'It's all about Implementation.' Without it,
the most wonderful idea is of little value.

STEP 7:
INSPECTION OF PROGRESS

At the end of the 6 steps to date there remains just a few more important processes that need to be put in place. These involve constructing:

- A plan for the follow up of individual initiatives, to either reward progress or correct lack of progress
- A system of measures that will enable you to monitor overall progress over the coming weeks and months

So the system of measures is tackled from two directions. Firstly, at the micro level, each of the initiatives that people are working on can be monitored to check that the plans are on track. At regular intervals these can be summarised and reported to management. Secondly, at the macro level, there are organisation level measures that will tell you how the overall project is going. The net profit as shown in financial accounts will be just one of these measures.

Tracking the individual initiatives

Some of the initiatives planned will have been taken on by people who have put initiatives into practice before. They will be happy to get on with the task and will report back to you at regular intervals. At the other extreme, some people will have done nothing like this before. They will need some serious support from you and others. They can be monitored as they are being helped through the process.

Soon after you start with this, it is an idea to split your overall list into 3 separate parts:
1. Initiatives completed in the last 12 months where the results are being monitored (the Inspection list)
2. Initiatives being worked on at the moment where results are being monitored (the Implementation list)
3. Initiatives that have not started yet which are at the planning stage (the Intention list)

There are clear advantages to tracking the progress in a rigorous way:

- It becomes easier to spot those initiatives that are not progressing as fast as they should be and be able to offer assistance
- Any resource issues can be addressed as soon as possible

For those who have not managed to complete their task - who present reasons and not results - engage them to find out what the real problems are and develop a solution.

There will be some initiatives that, even after your analysis of them as part of the last step, will not achieve what was expected.

Do not be afraid to call a halt to initiatives that are not going anywhere, although where this happens there should be a full explanation to everyone concerned.

Measuring the success
At regular intervals, perhaps once a month, the progress needs to be updated in the plan. How far through the project are they now? This can probably be estimated as a percentage of the total project. This time, the 'Increase in profits' is based on the actual increase achieved. This may be as difficult to measure as the original estimate, but it is worth going through those same assumptions.

As far as possible, the measures need to be easy to assimilate and track. Visual presentation, for example in graphs, works well.

- All current initiatives can be line-charted over time according to the percentage that they are complete
- Both completed and current initiatives can be charted to show their progress against the estimated profit increase in terms of value

Supporting the progress from the top
A review panel should be put together with the specific task of monitoring the progress of the initiatives. With a senior member of staff as the chairman, this should also include at

least one of the team leaders. This group should meet regularly.

In addition, 'Improvement progress update' should be an item on each management meeting agenda.

Unless the management visibly back the initiatives, then the interest and motivation of the individuals responsible is likely to wane.

Publishing the success
Positive feedback of results to staff is essential to keep the momentum. Any programme of this nature should have numerous successes. These must be made as visible and public as possible. You could have a special newsletter, articles in internal magazines, special meetings as well as using noticeboards and memorandums. Word of mouth is rarely enough.

The news should be focused on:

- Easy wins achieved;
- Milestones reached;
- Initiatives fully implemented; and
- Results achieved.

Success is part of the process and is important in ensuring continued confidence in the ongoing initiatives.

At least quarterly, if not monthly, these summaries should result in the rewards that were agreed in Step 2 being recognised.

Tracking the overall measures

At an organisation-wide level your regular management accounts should be able to tell you whether the entire exercise is working. There are always other factors that will influence this other than your 'Profit Improvement Project' work, so unfortunately you are unlikely to get the credit for all improvements. It is usually found, however, that the impact of the process is felt wider than just the initiatives being worked on. These opportunities to get people together will often mean that they work better as a team afterwards.

The key ratios that you identified as part of the work as part of the Information Gathering can continue to be tracked to see how they improve. Results need to be well documented, accessible, available quickly and positively described. At least some of these measures should be non-financial in nature.

There are often measures that provide an early indication of future improvements in net profit, such as customer satisfaction.

For example, customer focused ratios might include:

- Revenue per employee (net of returns)
- On time and in full order delivery
- Number of customers lost
- Number of customers gained
- Average customer age
- Value and quantity of returns/warranty claims
- Reputation in the marketplace
- Customer satisfaction scores

Employee satisfaction might be another area to monitor. If this is high or increasing then improvements in customer satisfaction and financial results usually follow. Intangibles such as this can be difficult to measure, but this can be done by creating 'opposite descriptions' for best case (scoring +7) and worse case (scoring -7) and asking the employees their opinion.

There is no need to monitor everything. Select the important measures to track and build up the history of them.

Congratulations! Everything is now in place. The only thing that is left for you to do is keep the momentum going over the coming weeks. This involves:

- Coaching all those who took responsibility for individual initiatives
- Monitoring the progress of initiatives completed and in progress
- Keeping the report on the agenda of management meetings
- Publicising and rewarding the success where initiatives have been completed

The secret now is consistency while the hard work continues to be carried out.

Final thoughts

You may be tempted, when going through this process in practice, to skip through stages to get some quicker results. To do so causes problems. For example, if you:

- Ignore the Introduction, then you will not be sure that the process is for you and your organisation
- Skip the Incentives, then you will face hard work later on and may never get started
- Avoid the Intentions, then you risk being confused, even heading off in the wrong direction and wasting time
- Miss the Issues, then you are unlikely to spot the real problems, which will continue to harm the organisation
- Ignore the Ideas, then everyone gets frustrated, especially if you know what the issues are
- Miss out on Implementation, then everyone has wasted a lot of time
- Allow the Inspection to lapse, then initiatives, especially the longer term ones, will lose momentum

So each stage is important in the journey and missing or skipping through any one of them reduces the chances of success.

A summary of the process

These are the Seven Immutable Laws of Profit Improvement.

1. Improving profitability will be rewarding, but is not easy. Make sure that you are prepared to go all the way through the process before setting out.
2. This is a people process. It is people who will make the difference between success and failure. Make sure that they will be properly incentivised before you start and broadcast these plans.
3. Make sure that you are in the right business in the first place before you go trying to identify improvements to be made. The process may involve you in moving in a different business direction altogether.
4. Identify the key issues that are holding the business back. You can waste valuable time tackling trivial matters.
5. Having identified the issues, your staff are likely to be the best people to be able to solve the problems. Get them together away from the business, achieve consensus on the solutions and capture the plans.
6. Never under-estimate the difficulty of implementation. Go through the Total Implementation Model for each idea if necessary.
7. Above all else, remember that Profit Improvement is the result of implementing ideas in a structured way.

PART TWO

PROFIT IMPROVEMENT
IN 227 ACTIONS

INTRODUCTION – PART TWO

This part of the book seeks to capture many ways in which all businesses could improve their profits and performance. Nobody can pretend to have captured all of the various ways that exist. There are many more that I know about that are specific to individual businesses and do not have general relevance across many sectors. This is why the **'Profit Improvement in 7 Steps'** was built around Action number 54 'Reward staff for good ideas'.

It is often found that the best ideas for improving profitability come not from an outside consultant but from the staff themselves. What is even more powerful is that staff then feel more motivated to do the really difficult thing and implement the good ideas that have been agreed.

In writing this I must acknowledge the inspiration and input of James Cross, originator of the Business Triangle concept. Having worked with this model for some time, I realised that the holistic business model that James had developed was analogous to the workings of the human body or, more accurately, the model of a human body in a state of peak fitness. At the beginning of each section into which the various ways have been analysed it will be demonstrated how the various parts of the sportsman at peak fitness is similar to a business that is at its 'prime'.

The ways have been split into three main categories, being the sides of James' model of a successful business, the Business Triangle. These are 'Management', 'Products & Services' and 'Finance'. We believe that for a business to be truly successful, it needs to be strong in each area and that major weaknesses in just one area will hold back the profitable development of the whole. You will see that each of these sections is further divided into three, so there are nine subsections in all.

When we asked small businesses to score themselves, we tended to find it was the 'Management' side that was the weakest.

Experience has shown me that there is something in here for everyone. Some of the ideas are unashamedly simple, because I often find that it is the simple things that get forgotten in the drive for growth or even in the daily grind.

This part of the book is hard reading if you try to tackle it in one go. It is best looked at in sections. At the end of each section there is an opportunity for you to score your own business on a scale from 1 to 10. At the end of the book you should be able to identify the areas that need the most attention.

You might also use this list in conjunction with Part 1 and issue it to staff just before the day set out in Step 5 – it helps to give them some ideas to get started with.

SECTION 1A:
MANAGEMENT – THE VISION

The Vision is as fundamental to a business as sight is to a human. You can get by without it but it makes things a lot more difficult. The better your eyesight, the further you can see, the better your opportunity of working out which direction you should be heading in and the more likely you are to be able to run in your chosen direction without bumping into something. This first section of tips looks at the ways in which the Vision of the business can be improved.

1. Develop a Mission Statement and communicate it

A Mission/Vision gives a business a mental focus and a sense of purpose. But that is not enough – it must be passed on to all who work in the business so that they too can have a clear sense of purpose and direction.

The owner can know where a business is heading but both customers and staff benefit from knowing as well.

2. Write a SMART business plan

This should cover the main functions like Marketing, Operations and Resources and so is much more than a financial document. It should comprise SMART objectives which are **S**pecific, **M**easurable, **A**chievable, **R**elevant and Time-based.

Your plan has more impact when written rather than in your head, but don't make it too long. Also avoid jargon and keep the assumptions realistic.

3. Make sure that a shareholders' agreement is in place

Cover the hard stuff such as what happens when one shareholder wants to leave and how the buyout price is to be calculated. The owners should vote unanimously for any change in future.

Businesses can easily lose the profit focus when arguments break out.

4. Recognise when a transformation is necessary

The bulk of the ideas in Part Two are small ideas leading to continuous improvement. Sometimes that is not enough and a major exercise is needed. A transformation covers a broad change in the business but takes some time to achieve.

Many successful businesses have needed to go through a transformation at some point. Nokia originally had nothing to do with mobile phones!

5. Prepare a rolling forecast instead of an annual budget

Cover the main headings and look for cashflow gaps that arise during the year.

Many budgets pass their date of usefulness during the year and software has made it easier to roll on a forecast.

6. Instil the profit attitude

Everyone on the business needs to have the profit attitude, not just the partners or directors. Ask the staff "What is your main responsibility?" and make sure that the response is "The profitability of the business".

If everyone feels responsible for profit, then it's more likely to be achieved.

7. Set targets higher than the prudent budget

Think of targets as a high jump bar and set them accordingly.

If you send your investors and bankers a prudent budget, giving these budgets as targets to staff means that you could miss some of their most profitable performance.

8. Develop the 'winners'

Business owners can focus the weakest sides of the business, but better results come by strengthening the 'winners'.

The winning sectors of your business do not always look after themselves. These areas are the ones where extra investment can reap the richest rewards.

9. Overcome resistance to change

Seek out the people who are stopping the business from moving forwards. Anyone in a business who resists change is like an anchor on a ship that is trying to move in open sea. Pull up the anchor to make more progress.

There are 3 things that make change threatening: surprise, usurpation and loss. People tend to view change in a personal way and find it hard to look from the business' point of view.

10. Acquire new skills or critical mass

This is usually a faster way to grow than aiming for organic growth. Sometimes the easiest and quickest way to improve profitability is to buy out the competition or bring in skills that are missing from the business.

The trick is not to quickly grow to a size where the management cannot control it and the entire operation suffers as a result.

11. Make alliances to move into new markets

Moving into an untried market is invariably a risky business. One way to reduce the risk is to move into new areas in alliance with another organisation that is not a competitor but has complimentary skills.

In a new market, an alliance gives you a head start, but choose your partners wisely and get the legal terms agreed early.

12. Build a franchise business

Alternatively, could you systematise your own business so that you can franchise it to others?

This takes a lot of work to get the system running but plenty of them make big profits for both the franchiser and franchisee.

13. Evaluate all new developments requiring investment

Costly mistakes can be made by allowing innovation to be king, no matter what the cost. Ask the right questions before things go too far – are they right for you?

New developments can be pursued without a clear idea of the benefits and suck up resources in the process.

14. Sell a non-core part of the business

Peripheral operations that do not contribute significantly to the main business ought to be divested.

Sometimes those 'hobby' businesses take up more management time than they are worth. Hard and emotional decisions often pay dividends here.

15. Walk the ship

Get out of your office and onto the shop floor where the action really is.

Many managers find that just by going out and asking staff "How is it going", means that they find out things about the operations that they never knew!

16. Measure performance regularly

Having set targets for staff (action 7), measure progress against them regularly. Monthly is fine, weekly is good and daily is even better.

What gets measured gets managed, and moved.

17. Incorporating feedback into the management process

Once the performance has been measured, complete the loop and use this information in the next budgets and targets. Sometimes it is the targets rather than the actual performance that need to be re-examined.

Improvement is iterative.

18. Opening up your books and accounts to staff

Staff like to feel 'in' on things. Particularly where the workers own part of the shares, this is essential. Staff must understand what the numbers mean if you want motivated performance.

Score 'The Vision' on a scale from 1 to 10   _____

SECTION 1B:
MANAGEMENT – THE PEOPLE

The People are situated at the 'heart' of the business and a strong heart is a prerequisite for a strong body. Just as the heart has four valves, so does the People side of a business - representing the four areas that need to be adequately covered. These are Technical, Marketing, Human Resources and Finance. Weaknesses in any one of these key areas, whatever the size of the business, means that the heart is not pumping as strongly as it could be.

19. Structure staff properly

On an organisation chart, clearly set out who is responsible for what area of the business, where are the lines of responsibility between them and who answers to whom? Then identify the gaps that need to be filled.

This should be set out even if there are just two people in the business.

20. Promote existing staff to fill vacancies

When the inevitable staff vacancies do arise, your existing, more junior staff should be considered first before looking outside the organisation.

External recruitment is expensive and risky. Internal recruitment is less so, as long as the existing staff have sufficient ability to be promoted.

21. Employ part-timers

Build up a database of flexi-staff who can work when needed. They can be more motivated to work harder than full-timers.

Part-timers should cost a business less in employment taxes.

22. Plan shift systems carefully

Care needs to be taken to ensure that the system does, in fact, increase output rather than reducing morale.

To maximise the running time in factories, shift systems are often introduced.

23. Utilise all the abilities of your staff

Ask staff to fill out a form listing skills, knowledge and areas of interest that are outside their job description and discuss how the use of skills benefits the company and them.

Employers are often surprised by the range of hidden and unutilised talents that staff have.

24. Offer flexible contracts

Most work needs to be flexible these days, to suit peaks and troughs of seasonality. If the work is flexible, offer an annualised contract that matches it.

Temporary workers can handle special projects or take up slack until permanent workers can be found.

25. Subcontract out under-utilised staff

If staff are not fully occupied at certain times of the year, but this is only a short term problem, can you subcontract the staff out instead of laying them off?

Maybe your customers or clients would find your staff useful on a short term contract?

26. Reduce overtime

Overtime is expensive when it costs more than the basic time. A full staffing compliment works out cheaper and better.

If staffing levels are always set too low, overtime can never be eliminated and staff will feel under pressure all of the time.

27. Smooth holidays throughout the year

If groups of staff take holidays at the same time, this puts strain on the remaining team and leads to more staff costs. Manage holiday planning in advance.

Particularly in smaller growing companies, the pressure on the staff can be intense.

28. Train staff to cover other jobs

In small staff teams, it becomes essential for people to cover each other in times of holidays and sickness. Train them in preparation for this, not after the event.

Especially in smaller businesses, staff will be pressurised at certain times of the day, week, month or year. But rarely is everyone busy at the same time, and those who see themselves as overburdened can be resentful.

29. Manage absence

Put the procedures in place to monitor and manage sickness. The first step is to ensure that it is properly measured on special absence forms, which allow the overall percentage to be calculated.

Absence from work constitutes a significant cost for most employers. Fixed overheads, and in many cases wages, continue to be paid. During sickness periods staff are making no contribution to the business and, in fact, may be doing more damage by upsetting production schedules.

30. Remove under-delegation

List all the things that you do and consider whether somebody more junior could be doing it instead. Then think about what your other staff are doing. This is a huge area where working could be much more efficient.

If this is happening it is a waste of talent and opportunity.

31. Form a round table of advisers

These will be people who do not work in the business but have experience, particularly in areas where you may be weak. Collect them once a quarter to share issues and plan actions.

Running any small business is a lonely job. Many owner-managed businesses are too small to be effective, probably representing only the owners and their family.

32. Use outside contractors for specialist skills

Specialist skills are expensive to acquire and, unless you need the individual all the time, this should be outsourced. An outside contractor is likely to perform better than less highly trained internal staff, so if specialised skills are needed a temp can do this better.

There are no holiday, sickness or training costs. Temps with limited responsibilities tend to be more productive.

33. Utilise the skills of non-executive directors

They will be particularly useful where directors have a strong hands-on style of management and may be unable to step back to look at the wider picture. They may be retired business people or experienced directors of other companies or academics.

The role of the non-executive director is to provide objective and independent advice to the other directors, but remain outside the normal day-to-day operations of the company.

34. Stop external recruitment

When someone leaves, do not automatically recruit a replacement. Justify the post and make sure that it remains necessary, given the passage of time.

It is easy to employ those extra people, but it is difficult to remove them! If people are like the heart of the business, then care must be taken to keep the right amount of pressure around it. Having too many staff can make the whole business lazy.

35. Install a people requisition system

This will identify the need and justify that recruitment is necessary. Appropriate authority levels can be agreed in advance.

Many businesses have an asset requisition system that ensures that every purchase of major capital equipment is justified. Very few have a similar system covering the addition of people, who are usually more expensive!

36. Recruit people who like people

Hire and retain people who will accept and enthusiastically carry out whatever is necessary to satisfy the customer, and thereby improve profitability. Make this one of your key recruitment goals.

"People do business with people" and these days most businesses are people businesses.

37. Offer staff recruitment incentives

Especially where staff are in short supply, consider offering bonuses to your existing staff members who successfully introduce new employees to the company.

Many businesses spend large sums for staff agencies to find permanent or temporary staff. Often their existing staff know friends and neighbours who would be interested. A financial incentive could save money immediately.

38. Induct new employees effectively

Make sure that everyone has a formal induction programme, geared to getting them familiar with their new job. What does a new employee need to know?

The first day at work should not be like the first day at school! A little extra investment at this stage pays dividends in the long run. In many cases a spell on the shop floor or in direct contact with the customer will be of benefit to management inductees.

39. Achieve the Investors in People award

Investing in people is a risk, but with people being one of a business' most valuable assets, many businesses have found that it pays to work towards the Investors in People award.

Companies need to maximise their investment in staff by ensuring that they make a real contribution to business success. It sends a positive message to existing and prospective staff and customers.

40. Get employees to write simple procedures manuals

A procedures manual is not to be confused with a job description, which sets out the duties to be performed by an employee. A procedures manual will explain how a job is actually done.

Instead of getting supervisors or consultants to write procedures manuals, get the staff themselves to write their own. They are better able to explain the job that they do so that others can understand it.

41. Use staff meetings as a training forum

If there is an external training course that would be relevant for a number of staff, consider sending only one person who is tasked with bringing back material.

Encourage staff to use the opportunity to pass on their knowledge to others. The spoken word is more readily understood than the written word. This will also improve the presentation skills of the presenters, so rotate the duties among the staff.

42. Align training with the business needs

Too many businesses put staff through training courses that are not necessary for them to do their job. Not enough time is spent at the planning stage to think about who are the right people for the training.

This wastes both time and money.

43. Assess staff objectively

Appraisal systems do not need to be extremely formal, but the larger the organisation, the more important it is that staff are assessed at least once a year. It is an opportunity for you all to step back, see the wood for the trees and review the year.

Appraisal systems do bring benefits, but they should be applied to as many staff as possible and not just the ones who are underperforming. Set down the criteria to make it clear what is expected.

44. Set staff SMART objectives

At regular appraisal sessions, make sure that the staff are set clear objectives that can be monitored at the next session. Failure to do this makes appraisals a waste of everyone's time.

Objectives set in this way have a much better chance of being successfully followed through, but only if they have been accepted by the staff member, rather than being imposed.

45. Manage out the weakest performers

While this is hard, there will be occasions when it becomes apparent that certain employees are not contributing to the business and may, in fact, be having the opposite effect. In these circumstances they need to be 'managed out' as painlessly and with as much dignity as possible.

The weakest performers are probably upsetting other staff and customers, so stopping the business from reaching its potential.

46. Relate pay to performance

Pay rises given at certain points in the year as a matter of routine should be stopped and instead be distributed to the most deserving candidates. This motivates them to continue and others see what is needed to emulate them.

Fixed bonuses equal fixed motivation and fixed performance; the best bonuses bring out the best actions.

47. Subcontract payroll to a bureau

All but the most complicated payroll functions can now be outsourced to bureaux that do this work all the time. They specialise so they are often more cost effective than doing the work in-house.

As payroll is normally a regular monthly operation, individual businesses will find it difficult to smooth the work effectively throughout a period.

48. Reward with benefits

Despite the fact that nearly all benefits now attract Employment tax for the employer, there is still some mileage left in benefits as part of the reward package. This is especially the case where a business can access a bulk discount for something such as health insurance.

Cash is not the only reward for good performance – and very often it is not even the most appropriate reward. Is there something else that people want?

49. Manage the use of cars

Changes in taxation have meant that company cars are no longer the benefit that they used to be. Generally where there is no necessity for a fleet it is much cheaper if the employee provides his own car and the employers reimburse business motoring costs with a mileage allowance scheme.

Many businesses provide company cars to far more people than can really justify them on good economic grounds.

50. Operate an effective pension scheme

Consider matching the employee's contribution into a money purchase scheme with an equal sum. Impose percentage limits that increase with age and length of service. This both limits your liability and more nearly matches the wishes of your employees.

It is estimated that 95% of workers are underfunded when it comes to pension provision.

51. Mobilise your workers

Interest must be generated at the bottom, by creating a groundswell which is guided by middle managers, who are in turn directed and coached by senior management, who are in turn led by the managing director.

Workers need to be prepared first before being encouraged to move together. Make sure that they know the Vision as part of the preparation.

52. Encourage teamwork

If your business is a rock, is everyone pushing in the same direction to move the rock, or is everyone pushing from different sides? Arrange regular social meetings and team briefings. Ensure that rewards are based on team performance rather than on individuals.

In a competitive environment, it is essential that the company works as if it is as one to beat its competitors in the marketplace. Departmentalism has to be eliminated.

53. Get rid of negative attitudes

These can infect an entire organisation. Firing the worst offenders works wonders for morale and allows good attitudes to work unimpeded. There is little point in having a polished product if it is sold by a surly and demoralised staff.

Attitudes are often formed at the top. If the manager is unhappy when he or she walks into the office, so is everyone else. Staff interpret actions and attitudes and copy them.

54. Reward staff for good ideas

This means following Step 2 of Part One of this book.

We find time and time again that staff are not asked for good ideas on a regular basis. Management is constantly surprised by the range and quality of ideas that staff come up with. Do you know the ideas that your staff have? Reward them for those ideas and they will be even better!

55. Reduce staff turnover

If the labour market is sensitive to changes in the rates offered, you should be able to proactively survey the staff advertisements. Small increases in the hourly rate can save large sums of money compared with the cost of someone leaving.

Staff leaving costs more than just recruitment costs. Think of training and lost management time for a start. Exit interviews can find out what the problems are.

56. Tackle stress in the workplace

Supervisors should be trained so that they can recognise changes in employee behaviour, and be aware of how best to approach the problem. This may also make supervisors more aware of the things they do that affect the stress levels of those under their supervision.

Put too much stress on the heart of the business and after a while the damage becomes clear. Don't let it get to the stage where the heart stops!

Score 'The People' on a scale from 1 to 10 _____

SECTION 1C:
MANAGEMENT – THE SYSTEMS

The Systems of a business are the glue that holds the business together, much like the way that our bone structure holds everything in place within our bodies. A break in a bone tends to slow movement and progress down and a break in your system will not heal itself without some intervention.

57. Invest in the right accounting package

Choose software that is adequately supported so that the problems that will arise can be solved for the foreseeable future. There are some more specialist packages for solicitors, farms or tyre fitters, to give but a few examples. These will be more expensive than the basic package but, being better structured from the outset, they should provide better results.

The right accounting package will give you sufficient information to manage your business.

58. Recognise the profit centres

This will involve setting up very detailed accounts ledgers and code lists. A first attempt at this project may, in fact, reveal that the existing accounting system is inadequate and that an upgraded system is required.

Break your business down into sectors so that you can work out which are the 'winners' and 'losers'.

59. Set up and monitor departmental budgets

Departmental budgets also provide the base material for fixing goals or targets for the individuals working in the department, and can form part of the basis for performance pay schemes.

Having worked out what the sectors are, allocate income and expenditure budgets so that you can monitor progress.

60. Develop flash reports

A flash report is a summary of key statistics which is prepared very soon after a period end. The numbers need to be easy to understand and so will be helpful in recognising trends. Where possible, record non monetary measures produced by the accounting system. This would include units sold, hours worked, etc.

Management and staff need certain information as soon as possible. If the full accounts take time to prepare, use flash reports to get key numbers to them fast.

61. Track key ratios

The benefit of ratios is that they can summarise key information in a single number, which avoids the need to draw information out of pages of material.

Every business has maybe five key ratios which determine the health of the business. Work out what they are and keep an eye on them regularly.

62. Fully integrate all business systems

Having an efficient accounting system is not sufficient; there needs to be an integrated strategy and management system so that there is a complete view of the business from the time that a potential customer is first identified to managing all the transactions until that customer finally leaves.

Many business systems have been built on a piecemeal basis. Unless they all fit together there is the risk that things can slip through.

63. Scrap wasteful procedures

Review all of your administrative systems for procedures that add no value and no longer have any purpose. Documenting them out in diagrams will help.

There is little more unprofitable than doing unnecessary work efficiently. With many businesses feeling that they are being strangled by external red tape, why make this worse by leaving your own red tape holding you back?

64. Restrict the opportunity for theft and fraud

Good physical and accounting systems can help protect against loss. However, it is just as important to have the right ethics and codes of practice so that everyone knows what is permissible, what is not and what the consequences of breaking the rules are.

Too many procedures and controls mean that staff will try to bypass them.

65. Ensure that all sales are invoiced

Overweight or over-volume deliveries give away the profit. Be under weight and you have broken the law. Be accurate and reconsider the way that you pack, price and sell goods.

Obvious, but easily overlooked; are all 'extras' agreed and charged for?

66. Limit the authority to spend money

In a purchase order system, should only senior management be able to approve orders or are you of sufficient size that you need to employ a purchasing manager? A purchasing manager can control the ordering system and will let everyone know that all purchasing must be approved, that this will be enforced and that they will not be paid unless they follow the rules.

How many times have you paid for something that you never knew had been ordered? By all means delegate authority to purchase, but set limits first.

67. Sign all cheques and contracts to see what is being paid

Test your system for controlling expenses by signing the cheques yourself. As you do so, look at each underlying invoice to see just what you are paying for.

It is not necessary to look at every cheque. Spot-checking has the same impact. It is also an idea to alternate cheque signers so that the responsibility is shared.

68. Have a disaster recovery plan in place

The objective is to provide a framework for responding to any eventuality so that the business could continue to operate with the minimum of disruption to its everyday activities.

Disasters can happen to anyone. No business can afford not to plan for the unexpected. At the very least plan how you would recover from the biggest risks.

69. Make more effective use of meetings

Set a limited number of objectives when planning the meeting. Make sure that a meeting is necessary in the first place, and consider whether a meeting is needed to achieve your objective.

Meetings cost time and money. If they are unsatisfactory and achieve little, they can going wrong before the meeting starts, during the meeting or after it has finished. It may be that it is best to stop them altogether.

70. Keep your staff informed

Communication cannot be left to chance. Employees need to be informed about what is happening in the business and why if there is to be a team spirit. It needs to be managed and the message needs to be controlled and consistent.

71. Ensure that all regulations are complied with

A tough one with the business environment becoming subject to increasing amounts of regulation and legislation, but a necessary one with each break in the structure slowing you down.

It is also becoming more evident that the penalties for breaches include the threat of fines to the company and even imprisonment of its directors and officers.

Score 'The Systems' on a scale from 1 to 10   _____

SECTION 2A:
PRODUCTS & SERVICES – THE SELLING PROCESS

The second section starts with one of the most important areas in any business. It can be argued that it is the customers who are the life-blood of a business and not cash or profits. Take the customers away or lose them and there is nobody to do business with! Just as an individual sells themselves through the image that they portray, every business has a selling process which, if there is a beginning and an end, starts with marketing and finishes in customer retention and referrals.

72. Keep track of the competition

Ask your customers about your competitors who are contacting them and see what they are offering them. If you have any new customers that you have won from the competition, find out why they left your competitor.

Winning the race is very much about being faster and better than the opposition. Where are they on the track and what seems to be their tactics?

73. Identify your niche in the marketplace

Having established what the competition is offering in your marketplace, it is easier to identify your company's niche by concentrating on your strengths and targeting where your competitors are weak.

Businesses start in a niche, but as they grow they lose focus.

74. Understand customer demands

Every potential customer is seeking a solution to a problem and if you are in business to provide those solutions you must communicate with your customers and potential customers to find out exactly what they need.

Very often the products and services that get provided are what we think the customer wants, when in fact they want and need something different.

75. Look after existing profitable customers

You should identify the 20% of your customers who are accounting for around 80% of your profits. On the premise that the existing customer base is one of your most valuable assets, the top 20% are the ones you need to concentrate on and nurture.

It is well-known that acquiring new customers is several times more expensive than retaining existing ones. It is easier to use your own blood rather than keep getting a transfusion! Very often, valuable customers get forgotten in the chase for new business and leave for a better service elsewhere.

76. Target new customers of high profit goods and services

High profit items make it worth seeking new customers who will be prepared to pay a premium price. They know that they need what you have to offer and there should be less competition.

Decide upon the best geographic areas and sectors to start with rather than spreading the message too thin.

77. Differentiate your product

The better the differentiation, the more difficult it is for consumers to decide solely on price, and the easier it becomes for you to be flexible with pricing based on the value that can be attached to the features or benefits being offered.

The product itself does not need to be any different from that supplied by your competitors, but it needs to be perceived differently. Your profits will not improve by becoming a 'me too' company, offering a product identical to those already on the market. If enough marketing imagination is applied, anything can be made to stand out from the crowd, but any differentiation you choose to highlight has to be both distinctive and valuable to the prospective customer.

78. Set business hours to suit the customer

Make it easy for people to spend money with you by being open when they need you.

Special needs warrant special hours and special prices! If you decide to adopt this policy, make sure your customers know about it.

79. Use an expert when exporting

This is a very specialist area. Many businesses have found themselves out of their depth when it comes to the customs and business practice in foreign markets. Experts in this area can save you a lot of time and expense.

Poor research and preparation have been identified as the main reasons for the failure of businesses that have experienced unsuccessful export ventures. Even when research is undertaken, it tends to be informal rather than professionally provided.

80. Treat suppliers as potential customers

Your suppliers can be an unrecognised source of new work and it should be easy to get an appointment, if only to drop in a cheque.

There can be hundreds of organisations that you do business with already who do not buy from you!

81. Calculate the lifetime value of new customers

Work out how much each customer is worth in monetary terms, and then calculate how much a marketing department should be willing to spend to acquire each customer. This tends to change the way that you judge your marketing effort.

If your customers are likely to be repeat business for you, they are worth a great deal more than is represented by the initial transaction.

82. Get involved with Trade Associations and Chambers

Take advantage of the services offered by these associations, such as industry surveys, group insurance, professional literature, education, a means to network, conferences and lobbying for industry, etc.

The emphasis is on being 'involved' rather than just turning up, so do something that you believe in.

83. Subscribe to the right organisations for the business

Subscriptions and donations are often paid because they were paid in the previous year. Ask for a list of such payments and establish which of them are worthwhile. Do any of these have any PR value, either internally with your staff or externally with customers and potential customers?

Capitalise on your generosity. It is easy to join associations for the good company, but make sure that the business benefits.

84. Talk to suppliers to get leads

Your suppliers may already be dealing with your potential customers. Better suppliers will be talking to all their customers in much the same way that they talk to you, trying to identify their needs to see if they can satisfy them. During the course of these conversations it is quite possible that needs will be identified which the supplier is unable to satisfy, but he knows that you can!

This extension of the relationship with a supplier becomes a two-way process with you giving leads to them as well.

85. Build a database of contacts and purging it regularly

A well-maintained customer database is a prerequisite for any business in its effort to improve the penetration of its sales to existing or new clients. Without it, opportunities will slip by without anyone realising it. Unfortunately the information is constantly eroding, so purging becomes a necessity.

A clean, accurate list increases your chances of a good response rate to any offer that you send out. Just one person should be 'Database Administrator', otherwise it never gets done!

86. Get everyone involved in the marketing of the business

If people believe that marketing is the preserve of management only, then opportunities are being missed. In most businesses, everyone has the opportunity to market the business that they work in, if only by portraying a good image of the business.

If it is not in the culture of your business for all people to be trying to get business for the firm, then you are missing out on perhaps the cheapest and most effective form of marketing.

87. Develop a SMART marketing plan

Like Business Plans, most Marketing Plans exist only in the heads of senior management, who may not agree. Put your SMART objectives down on paper and then communicate them internally.

By engaging in the practice of market planning, a company should be able to realise a return comparable or better than that of any other business investment.

88. Continue to market when things get tough

When a sector hits hard times, the businesses which tend to come out stronger are not those that cut back, but those which continue to market while others do not. They often set an objective of out-marketing their opposition and are rewarded accordingly.

Marketing is a strategic cost, but is similar to a lot of non-strategic costs that can be easily cut.

89. Share the costs of advertising

Very often your suppliers will be open to joint local advertising which markets both businesses. They may be agreeable to co-sponsoring events that will increase the profile with the target audience.

If you decide to use the backs of your vehicles creatively so that they can be read by the driver behind on our congested roads, consider using the rest of the space to advertise for your customers or suppliers.

90. Obtain references from satisfied customers

The best advertising is a satisfied customer. As your customers must be one of your most valuable assets, you can increase their value to you still further by obtaining references from them which they agree can be forwarded to potential new customers.

Your customers ought not to be concerned by your request, but should see it as an indication of your commitment to providing a high quality service to all your customers.

91. Take care of your reputation and image

If a company has a good reputation people will want to come and work for it, companies will want to supply it and customers will prefer to buy from it.

A good reputation generates reassurance and confidence, which translates into helping to sell more products.

92. Catch customers through your website

With 'the ability to order online' being one of the criteria which sets good websites apart from the average ones, there is still competitive advantage to be gained. However, not every product or service can be sold using e-commerce on the net.

Can you demonstrate that you are the expert in your field by publishing a 'White Paper' on your website?

93. Take every opportunity to get publicity

Articles in magazines and newspapers help to build awareness of your business and often can be placed without cost.

Many editors are looking for ready-made articles to put to newspapers. Modesty does not pay the bills.

94. Keep tabs on competitors' prices

You can either telephone them for individual prices, get a catalogue or send a member of staff to visit and make notes.

Before you can properly price your own goods and services, you must find out what your competitors are charging.

95. Price correctly

Price has nothing to do with cost. The right price for both goods and services is the highest price that the customers will pay, while some feel they have good value for money and being willing to come back.

It should not be your objective to be here today and gone tomorrow, with a trail of disgruntled customers chasing after you.

96. Be profit-driven and not sales-motivated

Applying the Pareto Principle (the 80:20 Rule)to your list of customers will have the effect of weeding out the least profitable customers, who are likely to be the ones not prepared to pay the price at which your profits are maximised.

Many businesses are sales-motivated by instinct, but often this means that they are not maximising their profits. Determine the likely effect of price rises on the business and adjust prices to maximise the profits. Owners' fears of a substantial drop in business are often unfounded.

97. Adopt target costing

As competition increases and supply exceeds demand, the 'cost plus' concept becomes more difficult or impossible to sustain. In these circumstances the basic equation changes to 'price – profit margin = cost', so that prices are driven by the market or the firm if it wants to increase market penetration.

98. Identify extra billing opportunities

Where has work been done that was in excess of an initial fixed quote? So long as these are identified early and explained to the customer, the extra fees for valuable work that you have paid the cost of can be billed and collected.

Don't leave extra profits 'lying on the table' - scoop them up!

99. Monitor enquiries and conversion rates

To develop an ongoing understanding of the success of your business, it can be important to register all significant enquiries that are received and track them through the system. Are there any trends that you can learn from?

Undesirable enquiries should be promptly refused and attractive enquiries pursued positively, while borderline cases should be pushed forward with caution.

100. Improve the proposal format

Proposals need to be clear and concise. Before a tender is finally submitted, it is imperative that it is meticulously reviewed. This reduces the risk that the contract will be unachievable and increases the value to the customer.

When tendering for business, write about the price first and the benefits last. The benefits will be the message that is left with them.

101. Follow up unsuccessful bids

Develop a questionnaire that is sent to all companies when they inform you that your tender has not been successful. They will often give the genuine reasons. You need to hear their opinions in order to make improvements that are likely to help when their next bid is needed.

Learn from rejection. The natural instinct is to shut failures from our mind and move on to the next project, but how are we to be successful at the next project if we do not know the reasons for losing the last one?

102. Be a customer-driven business

If customers are that fundamental to the health of a business, the only way to run a company properly is to decide what type of customer you want, what that customer's real needs are in the market, and then adjust your products, services, resources and costs to meet the needs of the market better than your competitors.

103. Aim to be 'much better than the rest'

The only way to achieve this may be through customer service, delivered via the effective combination of a well-organised, technologically advanced back office and a friendly, efficient front office. This can permit premium pricing.

This is no easy task. There is a Chinese proverb: 'It is harder to stay at the top than it is to get there'.

104. Keep the 'shine' on the product

You could make cleaning and tidying up part of everyone's job description?

There are many ways in which quality products and services can be compromised in short-sighted efforts to cut costs. You may get away with it once, but if it becomes a habit then customers can desert you for a better quality supplier.

105. Keep customers advised of progress

Letting people know the progress of their order gives you the best chance of getting a repeat order. There is a risk that next time they will try to find someone else who may be no better, but at least they are different.

If you can see the benefit in making this idea work, but the difficulty is in getting this type of service from your own suppliers, this could become one of your criteria in deciding who to do business with.

106. Use your website as more than an electronic brochure

Website development is concentrating on how the site can be used to gain extra business, or at least make it easier for your customers to do business with you.

Use expert assistance to implement Search Engine Optimisation techniques to place you above the competition in the listings.

107. Follow up previous customers

Identify good customers who have not bought from you for some time. Contact them directly to see if they are happy with their new suppliers and offer to visit.

Very often a telephone call can remind a customer that you are available and leads to extra work. It can also alter you to an issue that they have not told you about.

108. Find leads through your customers

Customers can help by providing a list of companies in their industry, introducing you to members of their trade association, or providing copies of their trade magazine.

Your customers are a qualified reference for your business and their opinion carries weight with their contacts. Asking is hard but usually rewarding.

109. Put yourself in charge of customer relations

Visit your current customers. Let them know that your job is to be sure that they are satisfied. You will attract more business because you are visible.

Do not assume that the customer necessarily wants the product that you provide at the moment. Use the opportunity to ask the customer want they want from your product and this will indicate the ways in which the sales lines can be broadened.

110. Actively seek feedback

Unless you actively seek feedback and obtain information from your customers you may not find out where you need to improve. More importantly, how will you know what goods and services that the customer needs are not provided at the moment (Action 76)?

A few companies may still believe that no improvements in products and services are required because they do not get any complaints. Smart companies are not so short-sighted.

111. Systematise the sales process

Having been through all of the above, now write down the best practice and learn from your best sales people.

The good advice needs to be passed onto the next generation.

Score 'The Selling Process' on a scale from 1 to 10 _____

SECTION 2B:
PRODUCTS & SERVICES – THE BUYING PROCESS

You are what you eat! A business consumes materials in much the same way and with the same effects you consume food. Eating the right type of food at the right time of day maintains peak fitness and maximises energy. Junk food is similar to poor quality materials – it causes problems later on. The next series of ideas suggests how you can buy the best materials from the best suppliers and have them there at the right time.

112. View the buying process as strategic

Supply shortages, the need to plan long-term for materials, a changing business environment, profit improvement through cost reduction and better use of purchasing talent have meant that buying which was previously done at plant or divisional level is now being centralised at the corporate level, because management increasingly perceive it as being important.

Group buying where possible is currently the order of the day to get all divisions in a group to use one supplier.

113. Develop better supplier relationships

Buying relationships have traditionally been adversarial. The focus tended to be on negative issues and was characterised by uncertainty. This was an inefficient relationship in which both parties missed out on opportunities. Major suppliers are being seen more as extensions of the customer's own organisation.

This type of new relationship involves considerable changes in behaviour and attitude in both the customer and supplier.

114. Agree exclusive buying deals

The rationale is, having selected a few 'preferred providers', they can be approached with the offer of an exclusive buying deal, which could guarantee business to a supplier in return for favourable prices.

It is sensible, however, to have a back-up supplier ready in case your primary supplier encounters difficulties of a more permanent nature.

115. Ask suppliers to help you reduce costs

It is becoming more common for people to ask their suppliers whether there is a cheaper alternative specification that fits the bill. Knowledgeable suppliers are often able to suggest alternative materials or less expensive processes. Consider your supplier as part of your process and integrate them.

Suppliers may even be able to carry out more of the process for you and improve the product at the same time.

116. Use credit cards for smaller purchases

Giving employees the chance to buy items might sound like a recipe for disaster, but once proper authority levels have been set, along with a rigorous system of checks, there are administrative savings to be made in this area.

Credit card payments can also be substituted for petty cash payments, which delays payment and reduces the level of cash that needs to be held and accounted for.

117. Plan purchasing needs ahead

Timely delivery of the goods and materials is needed to meet production programmes, sales plans and operating needs at a suitable price. Without sufficient time at the planning stage, problems are likely to arise later on.

An effective system will use the sales forecast to indicate the purchasing needs over the planning horizon.

118. Accurately specify the goods required

In a manufacturing company a single department may be responsible for specifications, but it must work in conjunction with marketing (who will know what can be sold), the purchasing department (who decide what can be bought) and the production team.

Of fundamental importance in purchasing is making sure that the right quality of goods, materials and so on is bought. If you ask for a steak in a restaurant, it is a rump steak or a sirloin steak and how do you want it cooked?

119. Include requisitions in the purchasing system

A requisition serves to initiate a purchase. For audit purposes it provides evidence of authorisation and action taken.

The purchasing department can be making purchases on behalf of production, sales or operating departments, but will rarely have the ability to determine what needs to be purchased. Therefore most purchases should be the result of requisitions from these other departments.

120. Don't always buy from the cheapest supplier

There is no good reason for always accepting the cheapest quote. Many people do not take the cheapest quote for work on their house because they are unhappy with the reputation of the builder or find that a more expensive quote more closely matches their requirements. The same is true when purchasing for a company.

Time is valuable and it costs money to sort out problems. Only buy cheaply if problems are unlikely or are outweighed by cost savings.

121. Put all major costs out to tender regularly

There may be good reason for dealing with regular suppliers for regular purchases but it is imperative to check the market periodically, just in case.

There are few costs that cannot be put out to tender. The frequency is a matter of judgement and will be influenced by the structure of the supply market.

122. Negotiate discounts

Seek discounts on virtually everything that you buy and then negotiate terms for payment and interest rates.

It may also be worth having someone scan the paid invoices file for discounts that were missed and should have been taken. Claim them!

123. Reduce order size unless a bulk discount is available

Generally the best run businesses keep their stock as low as possible to avoid tying up capital. They operate as closely as possible to a 'just-in-time' system. However there are occasions when it is worth increasing stock and the size of a purchases order when a truly unmissable deal comes along.

Sometimes there are good reasons for the availability of a deal. Goods shipped by the container load are often much cheaper and some businesses exist just to breakdown and sell on such bulk purchases.

124. Raise official order forms

In many cases both order and contract are incorporated in a single document, the purchase order form. All purchases, with some clear exceptions, should be made by this means.

Regular suppliers can be made aware of this rule by printing it on the order form or by stipulating that an order number must be quoted on invoices.

125. Specify a delivery time or schedule

The fundamental step in obtaining delivery on time is to decide exactly what is wanted at what time, to communicate this decision to those concerned and to insist that delivery is made at the time specified.

Very often businesses that complain of late deliveries by suppliers are themselves at fault for inaccurate delivery schedules or times that they have continually amended.

126. Have a simple small orders procedure

People requiring non-repeating small orders will generally know exactly what they want and where to get it. A simple cheque requisition form will be all that is required to cut out the invoicing/purchase ledger/payments procedure.

The administrative cost of the typical manual purchasing system can easily be disproportionate to the value of the order.

127. Monitor the progress of an order

Ensuring delivery on time can be difficult, particularly in certain industries. In such cases progressing an order, by chasing and following it up, is essential. For critical supplies you should check that the order has been received as soon as possible.

It is useful to provide space on the order form to record the progress.

128. Check the quality and accuracy of goods received

Checking the quality of the product received is the second stage of the purchasing quality assurance process. The first stage is the specification.

When you are buying fruit in a shop, you check it first before putting it in the basket. Some businesses who are lax in their checking only spot the poor quality at the end of the process. Too late!

129. Reverse the supply chain

Many suppliers will give credit for returns such as waste materials, product recalls, excess and faulty stock.

Don't throw it away when there's some value there.

Score 'The Buying Process' on a scale from 1 to 10 _____

SECTION 2C:
PRODUCTS & SERVICES – THE PRODUCTION PROCESS

The last part in this middle section was written for a manufacturing business, but many other businesses have a process in place to perform their work. One way of looking at a business' production process is to think about your own digestive system. Normally your food and drink works its way through the system and produces energy. Sometimes, the system cannot cope, and maybe the production process is not as efficient as it could be.

130. Review a number of manufacturing methods

There are usually several alternative methods of manufacturing a product. The choice depends on the trade-off between capital costs, operating costs and performance requirements. Do you look at all the alternatives regularly?

Time spent at this stage is probably a more valuable investment than the equipment itself.

131. Prepare an operating plan

In preparation for the drafting of the plan, a 'production stage chart' needs to be constructed. This will be able to predict delivery times following order, and may also determine the stockholding requirement and policy.

One hour spent in planning saves up to ten hours in execution.

132. Use standard items wherever possible

Purchasing ready-made parts is more attractive if there is a possibility of demand fluctuates or there is a risk of it falling off in the foreseeable future.

This also saves time and effort in designing and producing special items.

133. Remove any process that does not add value

Map out the process along the lines set out in Step 4 on page 46. Look for the places where there is waste. In practice the best procedure to follow is a basic problem-solving sequence. Brainstorming is used as a method of examination. The team suggests improvements using freethinking, with all judgments on ideas deferred until the consideration stage. This can sweep aside stereotype answers and come up with novel, original ideas.

If a process does not add value then it is unnecessary and a waste of resources.

134. Locate at the most cost-effective site

This will be influenced by the transport costs for raw materials and finished goods, availability of labour, delivery performance requirements and economies of scale.

Other factors include Government location incentives and local and national policies on issues such as building regulations, the environment and employment laws.

135. Simplify movement and handling of materials

Handling adds nothing to value, only to cost. In some factories the products can move many miles within the factory while no value is being added to them. The result needs to be supportive of group working, with adjacent tool racks, maintenance equipment and packaging materials. As far as possible, stores and storekeeping need to be eliminated.

Unnecessary movement is a waste of time and energy.

136. Support group working

Current wisdom is that there are advantages in assigning tasks not to a number of individuals, but to a number of teams. A small number of teams allows for a more modest investment in tools and equipment, while the problem of supplying parts and components is more manageable.

Team working is more flexible compared with a fixed production line, which is positive from the motivational point of view.

137. Improve working conditions and environment

You can improve the product and the production process so that the cost of production is reduced, but the job is not complete without some consideration of the conditions that people are working in.

Working conditions affect morale and performance. Fit the job to the worker.

138. Consider remote working

Developments in computers and communications are now such that many people can save commuting time and work from home. But make sure that your communication and team work is good before you try.

In the past, floor space was seen as an entitlement and as a status symbol (the more important you are, the bigger your office). This is now seen as an inefficient and expensive way of using office space.

139. Keep machinery as simple as possible

We may think that we are in an age where the faster and more advanced equipment is, the faster and cheaper the production process becomes.

But as with many things, when a simple machine does the job required, there is no point in acquiring an elaborate one.

140. Introduce technology in stages

The installation of a computer system can be a mammoth task, fraught with dangers and pitfalls, so they are best applied to the system in stages. The best place to start is stock control so that discipline can be established in this area first.

There are plenty of businesses who have ended up failing after installing a hi-tech system that did not perform as designed or expected.

141. Use technology to reduce costs or improve quality

Technology always opens up a wide range of possibilities and this can coincide with the markets becoming more demanding in terms of quality and variety of product.

The high investment of capital and other support needed for such systems demands high levels of plant utilisation and therefore longer periods of use.

142. Effective loading, scheduling and control

When work is correctly loaded, scheduled and controlled, optimum use can be made of capacity, completion times can be predicted and met, and urgent jobs can be given priority without upsetting the rest of the work.

Batches should be sequenced so that only incremental changes in machine settings are needed rather than jumps between extremes.

143. Adopt Just-In-Time as a total commercial strategy

The overall principle of Just-in-Time systems is that operations are not scheduled simply to keep people and machines busy, but that parts are made only when they are needed for the next manufacturing stage.

The aim is to use less human effort, equipment, time and space, while at the same time giving the customer what they want. The aims appear to compete, but they have been found to be complimentary.

144. Identify and removing bottlenecks

A bottleneck is any operation or activity where capacity is less than the current demand placed upon it.

The aim should be to get an order delivered as soon as possible after it is received because half finished goods are a waste. Apart from the obvious costs of handling, storage and interest, there is also the less obvious inertia imposed on the system by such holdings and the possibility that its presence can conceal shortcomings.

145. Control changes in specification

Especially when introduced in the later stages, such changes normally guarantee that costs in excess of the budget will be incurred. Sometimes these changes are unavoidable and have to be made for safety reasons or to solve an unforeseen design problem, but all proposed changes need to be controlled.

146. Monitor key information only

The first principle is to progress by exception. Highlight jobs that are running late.

Collecting a vast amount of information about jobs that are running to time may give people a feeling of achievement but does little real good. The trends may be more informative than the actual numbers.

147. Adopt a cradle-to-grave asset management strategy

In some ways cradle-to-grave is not an accurate description, given that the study ought to start at the pre-acquisition stage. Operation and maintenance strategies thereafter will be geared towards identifying the best use at least cost, and eventually a replacement or disposal strategy will be needed.

Life cycle costing involves equating the purchase, maintenance and disposal cost of equipment with the revenues generated and resale price.

148. Embrace total maintenance planning

Preventative maintenance is nearly always more cost-effective and less disruptive than repair or breakdown maintenance.

Breakdown maintenance is a waste of resources, lost contribution, wasted employees time, etc. The aim should be that the only unplanned time should be left for emergencies – and this should amount to no more than 10%.

149. Maintain a quality manual

A quality manual should set out the general quality policies, procedures and practices of the organisation. Decisions and guidance need to be given on when batches that fail should be rejected or reworked.

Quality specifications should be set at the design stage. The task for the operational side is to have all items leaving the factory meet this specification.

150. Monitor during the process, not just at the end of it

By catching the problem at an early stage it becomes easier to rework and if the item needs to be rejected and scrapped then at least the remainder of the process has not been gone through unnecessarily.

It can also be wasteful to check 100% of the work as it moves through the process. Usually some level of sample checking is far more effective and efficient.

151. Justify the warehousing policy

If you have your own warehouses, do you need them or is there a better way of organising the distribution of goods? It is dangerous to consider this in isolation from the rest of the process.

Many companies have carefully pruned distribution costs only to find that the savings have been offset by increased costs elsewhere in the business.

152. Utilise storage space efficiently

If you are starting with a green field site, building costs per cubic metre are at their cheapest between the heights of 6 and 15 metres.

The objective must be to get the maximum advantage from the given space.

153. Analyse the transport policy

The transport policy covers goods, materials and personnel, with the objective being to achieve a cost-effective operation that adds as little as possible to the cost burden on product prices.

If a fleet is needed but is not utilised, consider leasing out the drivers to other local businesses.

154. Plan loads and routes

Fleets need to be utilised as much as possible given the high level of standing costs in terms of depreciation, insurance and road tax. Therefore investment of resources in the effective planning of the loads and routes is generally well spent.

Costs can often be saved by having slightly fewer vehicles and/or drivers than required for occasional peaks, and hiring at peak times.

Score 'The Production Process' on a scale from 1 to 10 _____

SECTION 3A:
FINANCE – OPERATING ASSETS

The Operating Assets are the capital employed by the business in its operations. They include the various fixed assets as well as working capital. The better and more effective your utilisation of these assets, the more profitable you are. Think of your own limbs as an example of this.

155. Raise cash through a sale and leaseback

Could the capital that you have tied up in land and buildings be more effectively used to grow the business profitably? If the rental that you would pay is right, this is an option.

Substantial amounts of money can be tied up in these assets, which could be better spent and invested in other ways.

156. Generate an income from unused premises

The waste of spare space could be avoided by letting or sub-letting. Do suppliers or customers have a need? Otherwise there are lots of small businesses in need of space.

Sometimes businesses acquire more space than they immediately require to allow for future expansion. In other cases technology has changed the nature of the business or it has just contracted so that it has unused facilities.

157. Get at least three tenders for all major repairs

Major repairs, along with building and construction works in general, are one of the most important costs to put out to tender.

Quotes can be subject to quite wide variations depending on the methods used by the building firm and the materials to be used.

158. Negotiate lease costs attached to market value

Landlords normally structure their lease agreements so that rent reviews can trigger increases in the rent payable, but no reductions below the existing level. Negotiate a cancellation clause in the lease so that if business takes a turn for the worst, you will not be obliged to pay the unused term of the lease.

Unless the market is clearly booming, get as short a lease as possible.

159. Buy equipment wisely

If you have seasonal variations in the level of activity it is likely to be cheaper to hire equipment to meet the seasonal peaks.

Often there are items that are only rarely used. Amongst many other things to consider, only own equipment that meets the main needs of your business.

160. Consider short-term equipment leases

During the start-up period commitments should be as short-term as possible, at the expense of additional rentals if necessary.

If equipment is used for less than 60% of a year, it would probably be cheaper to lease it for that shorter period instead of a continuous five year period.

161. Keep lease costs under review

It is easy to acquire some equipment on an operating lease and then treat it like an owned asset, paying bills as they come in without looking at the alternatives.

Lease then buy can be the best option. If your existing machine is appropriate for your business and is near to the end of the lease, the best deal is struck by waiting until the end of the agreement.

162. Review maintenance contracts

These agreements can cost more than hiring repair or advisory services on an as-needed basis. If in doubt, use a few contracts as a trial.

Make sure that you are not continuing to pay for maintenance on equipment that has been scrapped.

163. Assess the optimum replacement cycle

Any replacement policy will be driven to some extent by the cashflow situation of the organisation, which should be flexible enough to take advantage of changes in the second-hand market value, or expected increases in the new prices.

For fleets of cars and equipment, keeping maintenance cost records will, over a period of time, allow accurate estimation of the point at which higher maintenance costs outweigh depreciation and other standing charges.

164. Sell assets not in use at market value

Cash that is released by a sale is surely preferable to an idle asset. If it is being financed there will be a penalty to pay, but if the sale generates enough to clear this, the other hidden benefits can be realised. Even assets that are fully paid for can be a drain on profit, particularly when it is not fully utilised such as a pool vehicle, vacant land or office space, or old machinery.

Remember to sell for their market value, not the book value!

165. Develop a stock control system

Good stock control and ordering systems are the key to avoiding stock build up in the first place and spotting problems quickly.

Set minimum and maximum stock levels for each line.

166. Liquidate old or obsolete stock

It is estimated that the hidden costs of holding stock can be 2% of its purchase cost per month. Sell old and obsolete stock, realise what cash you can and use the capital more wisely.

Old stock is a liability not an asset!

167. Reduce the number of stock lines

Where the differences between lines are nominal, work out which is the more profitable and stop the production or purchase of the other ones.

One of the main causes of stock and work in progress being higher than is necessary relates to the variety of products sold. The more lines that a company has, the more stock is needed. Most business finds that 80% of the stock is producing only 20% of the contribution.

168. Purchase on sale or return where possible

Suppliers may demand a premium price for keeping this risk, but in a changing market this may well be worth it.

You have to ask for it and it helps if you are a key customer.

169. Subcontract out non-core processes

The investment in any process in terms of labour, materials and equipment has to be justified and weighed against the normally preferable alternative of buying in the ready-made finished article from elsewhere.

If a process is non-core to the business, why is it being carried out in-house at all?

170. Set up credit practices

For a start, make sure that your Terms of Business are included on all documentation, including quotes. These must be as clear as possible, so that the person reading them, which may be the courts, is in no doubt as to what is intended.

Poor credit policies are a prescription for trouble in any company and in any economy.

171. Take up credit references regularly

The principle should be extended to existing customers as well. Are they still as healthy as they were when you started doing business with them? If not, then be selective about the amount of credit that you offer them.

Many credit scoring providers now monitor up to date payment records as well as historic accounts and they will now alert you when the score of a company that you are monitoring changes.

172. Encourage customers to pay by credit card

This speeds up the collection of debts by turning what would otherwise be 'credit sales' into the equivalent of cash sales.

If all your account customers paid by credit card, wouldn't it be worth paying the charges to avoid the risk of late payment and bad debts?

173. Agree an invoicing and payment schedule

Wherever possible, get the customer to sign a contract or engagement letter that sets out the stages at which invoices are to be presented and paid. As part of this, they can agree that they will be liable for any costs incurred in collecting the debt should this become necessary through late payment.

Make sure that a due date is obvious on all invoices and statements.

174. Offer discounts to encourage prompt payment

Consider offering discounts if people pay before the end of the normal terms of business. There will be a tendency for customers to take this discount whenever they pay, so introducing this type of discount requires close monitoring to make it clear that the terms must be adhered to, otherwise part of the debt remains outstanding.

The improvement in the cashflow may well be worth the cost to the company, but make the comparison before you make the offer.

175. Invoice as soon as possible after sale

Be very prompt in sending out invoices. Failure to do this will give the impression to debtors that you do not mind how long you wait for your money!

Make sure that invoices go out at least 7 days before the month's end so that they get in the current month's payment cycle.

176. Stick to collection practices

Once you have set up your credit practices, the next stage is to ensure they are implemented. Your customers have no grounds for complaint if they have agreed to payment terms when they placed the order.

The slower paying an account becomes, the more difficult it is to collect.

177. Help your customers to pay promptly

Send out statements twice a month and provide an envelope for payment by return. This will entail a little more work and cost but the benefits can be significant. There is nothing sacred about sending statements out only at the end of each month.

Put as much information as possible on the invoice and statement to eliminate potential problems and delays in payment.

178. Invoice accurately

One of the most common excuses for failure to pay an invoice is that it contains errors or that the invoice does not accurately explain the goods or services provided. Payment will be made only when these problems are rectified to the satisfaction of the customer.

Ideally follow the sending of the invoice up with a quick telephone call.

179. Charge penalties on late paying accounts

To do otherwise puts your good customers at a disadvantage relative to your bad customers. Make sure invoices and statements indicate when the payment is due and what penalty will be imposed if the payment is not on time.

The penalties need to be applied as stated, otherwise they will eventually have no effect and customers will continue to delay payments.

180. Chase bad debtors yourself

Persistence pays. There are courses available that will tutor your staff in the practice of sending official letters that escalate in severity and the process of taking people to Court. Usually a visit is more effective than a string of letters, emails and telephone calls.

Solicitors and debt collection agencies make a good living when customers do not pay.

181. Take full advantage of discounts offered

After the quantity discount has been agreed, ask for a prompt payment discount. A 2% discount for paying 20 days early is the equivalent of earning 36% on your money in a year.

When in doubt, take the discount even if you are paying a few days past the due date.

182. Pay invoices when they are due

Invoices should be categorised by their due date so that they are paid in order. As an alternative, pay invoices as soon as they are approved. Then there is no need for a purchase ledger, with its associated costs.

Amounts owed to suppliers appear as a liability in the accounts, but if they are providing you with credit, then they are an asset. Don't crucify suppliers in order to conserve cash.

Score 'Operating Assets' on a scale from 1 to 10   _____

SECTION 3B:
FINANCE – OVERHEADS & TAXATION

The biological analogy works especially well here. Think of overheads as the layers of skin and fat that you carry. You need a certain amount but not too much. Do not be a victim of corporate anorexia!

183. Task a committee to cut costs

On the basis that staff have different perspectives from the owner, they will have some interesting and beneficial ideas. Ask for volunteers and recruit three people. Require a written report suggesting ways to eliminate or reduce costs.

Even when things are going well the staff will have good ideas on how to improve them further, as they will be closer to what is really happening on the ground.

184. Outsource support functions

Decide which operations are suitable for outsourcing. Then set appropriate performance and cost comparisons to assess supplier bids.

This is becoming more prevalent as more businesses recognise the need to strip out internal functions that prevent them from concentrating on their core markets.

185. Keep a tight rein on office supplies

Most offices have piles of unused stationery and forms. If you opened all the desk drawers and valued the unused stationery in there, how much would you find?

Declare an amnesty for returned supplies then lock the stationery cupboard.

186. Monitor the use of phones and the internet

Check unusually long calls, especially to mobiles, and see if there is any way that they can be made shorter. It is not only the outgoing calls that need to be monitored but the incoming ones as well. Monitor internet usage during work hours as well.

Each member of staff can therefore be provided with a printout of their calls made in the last period, which acts to deter private usage and target reductions in the overall bill.

187. Try mediation before litigation

A litigious attitude can cause more problems and difficulties than it solves. Make sure that contracts are drafted including an arbitration clause.

Court action in complex cases can run into many figures. Few businesses can afford even to consider this.

188. Get experts to check the rates paid

Instead of tying up large amounts of your staff's time, it makes sense to contract a specialist in cost reduction.

Make sure that the organisation is reputable and will be paid on results, not their time spent.

189. Develop an energy management programme

Everyone in the business should recognise the importance of energy conservation for the benefit of the environment as well as the company. Rewards for notable conservation efforts will help to broadcast the message.

Saving money is not the only reason for cutting energy consumption. It is also the most cost-effective way of tackling the threat of global warming.

190. Check the accuracy of bills

Make sure that you have received what you are paying for. Every invoice should be checked by the right person.

Everyone makes mistakes.

191. Make your staff responsible for conservation

Before you can motivate staff to stop wasting energy, you will need to raise their awareness of the benefits and effects. They need to see that energy efficiency delivers tangible rewards to them.

When put in concrete terms, energy saving initiatives are usually welcomed by the staff, as energy efficiency is equally relevant for the home. Employees can be shown how to use the same practices at home to cut their own bills.

192. Keep energy contracts under review

Many businesses now have fixed term contracts that need to be reviewed in good time, otherwise you can carry on paying an uncompetitive rate. Monitor the needs and usages of different sites to compare the different tariffs that will be used.

The price of energy continues to fluctuate and has to be monitored.

193. Carry out an insurance risk audit

By analysing the probability and potential severity of loss, and the scope for reducing these, an action plan for the management of risk can be drawn up.

Insurance can instil a false sense of security – unsatisfactory risk features may be overlooked if comfort is taken from a possible insurance recovery in the event of a loss.

194. Ensure your broker goes to tender

The onus falls on you to check that they are shopping around on your behalf, especially if you have been dealing with the same insurance company for a number of years.

Be careful not to have too many brokers checking the market for you. The insurance companies will wonder why and increase quotes accordingly.

195. Co-ordinate renewal dates to catch duplications

Many businesses waste a lot of money because they have unwittingly duplicated unnecessary or obsolete insurance coverage.

Look out for idle and seasonal equipment on which insurance can be suspended, or equipment that you no longer own. Also check for equipment where the insured cost is more than the replacement cost.

196. Run a driver training programme

If you have a bad accident record you could charge the insurance excesses incurred to the drivers at fault, but this will not tackle the root cause, which may be that drivers are inexperienced and need some training. Some ex-police officers provide this.

If your claims are low consider the impact of increasing the policy excess for car accidents and contents.

197. Rationalise the company car fleet

With the taxation of company cars seeming to increase each year, it could be much cheaper for the employee to provide his or her own car and be reimbursed business motoring costs with a mileage allowance scheme.

Businesses with salespeople who travel high mileages and likely to need a fleet of company cars, for them the question is how to provide the cars at the lowest possible cost.

198. Have a written policy for travel and entertainment

Have a published policy covering all travel expenses. Fix entertainment allowances both for an individual item and in terms of total annual expenditure.

Business entertainment expenses can be money well spent if new business is gained, new contacts made or old ones reinforced. Make participants report on the benefits they obtained and the business done at each such event.

199. Bring training to your staff

There are occasions when the speaker can be brought to you. Otherwise get those who attend seminars to present the key messages to the rest of the staff.

Use the seminars of the local association's group to provide a core training programme that covers ongoing issues and then cover specialist areas on an individual basis.

200. Use video conferencing

Video conferencing for corporate meetings is now with us and the cost is reducing. How much travel time could you save?

201. Get previous tax payments refunded

Both companies and unincorporated businesses can set a tax loss against immediate past profits and get a refund during the year of the loss.

Do not let the Government hold onto your money.

202. Arrange a tax planning session before each year end

Meet your tax adviser about two months before a year end so that you can take advantage of any tax planning opportunities. Little can be done after the year end.

Any company looking to reduce its overall tax burden should ensure that it is adopting best practice before looking at intricate tax avoidance schemes.

203. Extract profits effectively

The extraction options could include remuneration, dividends or benefits.

The best solution can change as each tax year passes.

Score 'Overheads & Taxation' on a scale from 1 to 10 _____

SECTION 3C:
FINANCE – CASH & FUNDING

The last section of this book covers the life or death subject of money. Cash flows through the business like blood through a body. If you lose too much too quickly then your business is at risk! Make the most of what you have and invest the balance wisely until it is needed.

204. Approach financiers with solid proposals

Make sure that you understand the information that the bank wants. This normally extends far beyond a simply financial projection and includes an appreciation of the business, its management and the key people involved.

The better the application the greater the chance of overcoming the hurdles. Banks are now organised so that the manager is not likely to be the person to authorise the lending. The better their understanding of your proposition, the better the quality of the case you give to them, the easier it is for them to be a good representative.

205. Produce rolling cashflow forecasts

These forecasts should not be produced just to accompany the annual budget. If you prepare and update them at least monthly they can be an essential tool in keeping on top of future financing needs.

They should highlight cash problems at an early stage and allow plenty of time to arrange a facility before it is needed, and not when the business is desperate.

206. Be honest about financing problems that arise

Bankers do not like surprises! They prefer to hear about problems as soon as possible – while it is still possible to act positively. Agree to share results with your banker on a monthly or quarterly basis.

After a banker realises bad news has been suppressed, it is human nature for them then to wonder "How much else have I not been told?"

207. Investigate the availability of grants

You may be able to get grants or cheap loans from a variety of sources, but make sure that the time and effort involved is likely to be worth it.

Project grants can be related to the fixed and working capital costs of a project and to the number of jobs it is expected to safeguard and/or create in the assisted areas, normally within three years of the project start.

208. Match the funding with the assets

The difference between peak and minimum borrowing requirement represents the short-term funding requirement and an overdraft will be the most appropriate form of borrowing. The remainder is 'hard-core' borrowing which should be split between medium and long-term, depending on the asset that is being financed.

Care needs to be taken when choosing between different types of financing on offer and a package needs to be tailored to the individual business requirements.

209. Fit lease payment terms into the business cycle

Many banks and leasing companies offer flexible plans so that payments can fluctuate to match cashflow instead of being on a simple straight line basis. It is also possible to include an initial repayment holiday.

210. Have contingency plans at all times

Consider the implications of not receiving any cash for the next 60 to 90 days, or if interest rates went up by 5%, or if the bank wants to reduce the facility. How would the business survive? If the answer is not apparent then a plan is needed.

Having done this you are prepared to react quickly and appropriately if something does not go as planned.

211. Protect key employees with Keyperson insurance

The proceeds of a policy would allow the business to fund the recruitment of a replacement. Which of your employees are that critical to the business' success?

Sums insured need to be monitored at each renewal. In a growing company, each person's value may also grow. Regular medical check-ups are a good discipline for both the employer and the employee to monitor health and courses in stress management and relaxation are useful.

212. Keep investments within easy reach

If there is a risk that the business could suffer a downturn, surplus cash should be on short term deposit rather than invested for the long term.

Cash is King. If there is sufficient contingency built into the forecasts, put the balance into a higher interest account with a notice period of up to three months.

213. Shield personal assets from creditors

Only give a personal guarantee if it is absolutely necessary and agree the terms of their discharge before they are given.

If your spouse has no interest in your business, there is no reason for a bank to request that him or her sign as guarantee for a loan.

214. Refinance to reduce interest charges

Review interest costs on all debt. If a loan was taken out to finance a new and possibly risky project, the bank is likely to have reflected this in a higher interest charge. If the risk is now lower this could be reflected in a lower interest charge.

Banking costs can be put out to tender like the majority of other costs with the result that you could get a better interest rate on long-term loans and a more competitive spirit from your bank.

215. Hedge against interest rate risk

Rates have always been difficult to predict, such that significant adverse swings can make the difference between solvency and receivership. If you borrow large sums of money, consider some protection against large jumps in interest rates.

For the most part rates have become difficult to predict, both in their timing and in their magnitude, such that significant adverse swings can make the difference between profitability and loss making.

216. Use surplus cash to reduce loans

As the cost of borrowing exceeds the return on invested idle funds, if you have cash available it makes sense to reduce the company's debt. However, pay off debt in a sensible order and consider the future cashflow of the business.

217. Negotiate credit card collection fees

With most processing now online, the factors are the number of transactions and the monetary amount. If these have grown significantly since the rate was agreed, then it would be worth negotiating a reduction in the processing fee.

It pays to shop for the best deal.

218. Automate the payment system

Bank charges for processing manual cheques have multiplied in recent years, while direct debits are free. Calculate how much could be saved by using an Electronic Data Interchange (EDI) system to transfer the funds instead.

By using EDI rather than the postal system, companies are able to manage their cashflows more effectively and be in a position to negotiate better discounts with suppliers by demonstrating that cleared funds will be available on the promised day.

219. Check the bank's calculations

Banks make mistakes! The miscalculations of the clearing banks have continued even though computers have become more sophisticated.

Computer packages are available to do the checking for you, otherwise there is likely to be a retired bank manager who can do it instead!

220. Carefully choose where to bank large amount of cash

If you get a lot of receipts in the form of cash, rather than cheques or credit cards, it is worth investigating the rates charged. Not all banks charge for this.

221. Bank cash and cheques daily

If you do this, cash balances will be earning the maximum interest and overdrafts will be suffering the lowest interest; accounting and accounts receivable records can be kept up to date and cheques and cash are less likely to go missing.

Bank cheques immediately, even if you are unsure of the customer account to which they relate. These can be photocopied for reference if necessary and followed up later.

222. Be linked directly to your bank's records

This means that your cashflow can be monitored daily.

Account data flowing in from the bank and payment data flowing out to the bank can be integrated with a company's accounting system, so that data is only entered once.

223. Move surplus cash into overnight deposit

This means that interest can be earned even on money for which a cheque has been written but not yet presented. Truly surplus cash is usually better invested elsewhere.

224. Arrange to receive money through the BACS system

By encouraging your customers to do this it is possible to have money credited to your account a few days earlier. The days saved are generally those in which the cheque is in the post or in the banking system. Also, BACS payments are less likely to be misappropriated like a cheque.

These credits are generally free of charge as well.

225. Use your overdraft facility

Having negotiated an overdraft facility, perhaps as a safety net, it is important to use it at some point during the year. If not, the bank could argue that the facility is not necessary and cancel it.

Some of the ways of achieving this are the reverse of advice given elsewhere in this section!

226. Manage currency risk

Having a currency account enables the business to bill in that currency, taking funds into that account which can be applied to pay for purchases from that country or, should rates become favourable, converting into sterling.

The continuing volatility of exchange rates makes the management of the currency risk a priority. Minimising the impact of these risks contributes to the short-term stability of the business, and to the long-term financial planning and development process.

227. Avoid withdrawing all of the surplus funds

Businesses need adequate working capital to take advantage of the opportunities that many of these actions entail, so the last thing that you should do having made lots of extra profit is then take it all out of the business.

Your body cannot function and rapidly deteriorates if it loses too much blood, and your business cannot function properly if you starve it of cash.

Score 'Cash & Funding' on a scale from 1 to 10 _____

Congratulations! You have made it through all of the 227 actions.

Revisit your scores in each section. The section with the lowest score should be the place to start.

In the A to Z of Profit Improvement, 'A' stands for 'Action'. So it's now time to move on with the implementation, which means referring back to Step 6 in Part One.

ABOUT THE AUTHOR

Tim Levey is a Partner and Head of Business Consulting at Reeves, a Top 30 Accountancy and Financial Services practice in London and the South East of the UK.

He is the author of:
'Profit Improvement in a Week' which was published in 2004 by Hodder & Stoughton;
'NEVER Cut Costs…….' which was published in 2010 by Perfect Profit.

For further information of Reeves' services, visit
www.reeves.co